Whale Tales

Human Interactions with Whales

volume one

HELEN + DAVID —

I HOPE YOU ENJOY

WHALE TALES —

Peter Fromm

6/02

Whale Tales Press · Friday Harbor, Washington, USA

Whale Tales Press
PO Box 865 • Friday Harbor, Washington 98250
360/378-8378

Front cover photo ©1989 Alan Cortash. Kelley Balcomb-Bartok sharing an illustration with Hyak at the Vancouver, B.C., Aquarium. See: "Pictures For Hyak," page 11.

Back cover photo ©1993 Carol Miller. Touching a friendly gray whale, San Ignacio Lagoon, Baja California, Mexico. See: "Friendly and Not So Friendly," page 46.

Original illustrations for Whale Tales ©1996 by Kate Scott and ©1996 by Julie Gomez. Whale Tales tail logo © By Design, Friday Harbor, WA. Kate's work appears on pages 5, 25, 41, 66, 76, 86. Julie's work appears on pages 19, 51, 124.

"Contact Made" ©1995 Ross Isaacs, Ocean Planet Images®. Used by permission.

Whale Tales was originally designed by Ian Byington of By Design • Friday Harbor, Washington 98250, and redesigned in 2000 by Bruce Conway

For ordering information,
please call: **1-800-669-3950**
Quantity purchase discounts are available.

Please contact Peter J. Fromm through Whale Tales Press to schedule speaking/reading engagements or multimedia presentations.

Printing history: First printing, November 1995
Second printing, July 1996
Third printing, November 2000

Library of Congress Cataloging-in Publication Data
Fromm, Peter J. (1947 -   )
Whale Tales: Human Interactions With Whales, Volume One
Collected By Peter J. Fromm

Includes index.
ISBN 0-9648704-0-1
1. Whales   2. Whale—World   3. Folktales—Whales   4. Interspecies
Communication   II. Title
LOC Catalog Card Number 95-90817

Manufactured in the United States of America.

Dedication

For the people working to return Tokitae
("Lolita" at the Miami Seaquarium) home to J-Pod,
her family in the Pacific Northwest.

Thirty years in jail, for being a pretty whale,
is long enough.

Imagine what a greeting ceremony she will have.

Imagine what tales Tokitae will tell about us.

Bring this long-lost sister home.

Whale Tales
Human Interactions With Whales

Orca Tales

Minke Tales

Humpback Tales

Gray Whale Tales

Sperm Whale Tale

Whales Come To Boats

Swimming With Whales

Feeding The Animals

Collisions

Research

Calling The Whales

Dying Whales

Rescues

Appendices

To the Reader

by Peter J. Fromm

It is estimated that whale watching businesses worldwide today generate as much, or more, income than the whale killing industry did at its height. After more than eight hundred years of commercially hunting whales; people are now mentally, emotionally and spiritually moved by being close to these animals. For some reason, human lives can be positively changed by interactions with whales. I have seen this happen many times in three years of working as captain and naturalist on a whale watching boat.

Something powerful happens when these marine mammals look you in the eye. Their brains are as large and complex as ours, and one senses it fast. Many stories in this book speak of this.

Whale Tales came from all sorts of people, doing a wide variety of things, all over the world. It was important to me to include biographical information about the contributors so you know who is telling the story. I enjoy the notion that this book is much more folklore than either science or literature.

It has been a tremendous amount of fun to produce *Whale Tales*. This has been the most exciting thing I have ever done.

I had not intended to include any of my stories in this first volume. I thought I would save my experiences for a later book. As Fate would have it, within twelve hours of writing those words, I had an encounter to share.

In January, 1995, one year after the conversation which launched this "I'm going to make a book about human interactions with whales" journey, I was out on my boat working on the book. I had just begun to motor the seven miles back home. It was a gray morning: flat, glassy calm water, with a low cloud cover. Driftwood was floating all over the place, winter high tides pulled it off the beaches of the San Juan Islands of northwestern Washington.

As I looked ahead to find my way through the flotsam, I spotted the dorsal fin of a male orca! I was surprised and quickly looked around; four other fins broke the surface and disappeared. I was with J-pod. What a treat!

I traveled with these twenty two whales, including two babies less than a month old, for two hours. There were no other boats out that morning. I placed one of the stereo speakers by the hull of my wooden sailboat and turned up the volume. King Sunny Ade's "Live, Live JuJu" tape was on; lively African drum and guitar music. About every ten minutes a whale or two would spyhop and look right at my boat "Uwila," as if to see where the music was coming from.

At one point, the entire pod went into "resting" mode. All the orcas were just logging around on the surface by themselves or in small groups. I shut off the motor and drifted with them. J-One, Ruffles, a large male I have taken some nice photographs of, and the first whale I spotted that morning, surfaced about forty feet away. He lay there resting for ten minutes. His breathing sounded like someone snoring. Then he awoke and the pod began moving again.

As I motored towards Lopez Island, the whales swam in a long line towards Cattle Pass at the end of San Juan Island; we were in a crossing pattern. One or two at a time, every orca in J-pod surfaced within twenty feet of me. A state ferry went by, and all the passengers were out on deck to see the orcas. One of my friends, Michael, was on board. He later told me that if ever there was a "sign" about the rightness of something, there it was. It seemed to him that the whales were checking with me to find out how *Whale Tales* was going.

There might be even more to it than that.

Peter J. Fromm
S/V "Uwila"
San Juan Islands, Washington
September, 1995

Forward
by Ken Balcomb

There are very few people who are not swept with excitement in the presence of leviathan or its diminutive cousins in the watery world of their domain. That is almost routine, and it requires only a whale watching trip to verify it for yourself. But there is often something more about this cetaceous presence that requires explanation and further description, albeit subjective at times.

Humans, masterful as we are on land, are relatively inept when it comes to propelling ourselves unassisted through the ocean, or even lakes, streams, or a swimming pool. We can barely imagine what goes on in a whale or dolphin's life at night or in the invisible depths of the sea. Much less do we know what goes on in its head. So, do we make up what we cannot see, or otherwise know? Not in traditional science or quest for knowledge. For the most part, we know only that they live their entire life in an aquatic mode, remote from our view and evolutionary experience. Out of occupational necessity, or out of curiosity, many of us find ourselves out on the ocean one day; and, suddenly we are presented with a most amazing experience that only these cetaceous beings can offer. And then, who do we tell? Who would ever believe it?

Having spent many years at sea, and having had or witnessed others having some of these amazing experiences, I am quite delighted to see a collection of these first-person narratives made available to a broad audience. You can take them all with a grain of salt, if you wish; but, collectively, they paint a most interesting picture of our earthly relationship with cetaceans.

Anthropomorphics aside, let's say that all of the authors were describing their experiences with Martians. Wouldn't it be fair to say that most felt the contact was with another sentient and intelligent being? Was this feeling predisposed by our cultural bias which has placed the whale and the dolphin on some sort of spiritual pedestal, or was it something the animal did that made it seem sentient and intelligent? Given the broad spectrum of the authors' backgrounds, I'm inclined to think that the essential part is something that the whale or dolphin did. I cannot begin to explain why, but I get the sense that they are very aware of us as a fellow earth being, that they are mutually aware of this even across species, and on the whole, that they are toying with us. It will be interesting to include your thoughts and experiences in future volumes of *Whale Tales.*

Ken Balcomb
Center For Whale Research
Friday Harbor, Washington
August 1995

Introduction
by Rich Osborne

The origins of what we now call Natural History probably began as simple stories among friends and relatives about what was experienced in encounters with nature. These stories, the oldest of which perhaps originated sometime during the Pleistocene epoch, must have gone through their own process of natural selection, where the descriptions of average experiences became common knowledge, and the unique and fantastic stories became the fodder for long-term oral traditions. So in old science the oral traditions tended to survive the longest and the original common knowledge tended to become lost.

One of the most powerful aspects of modern science is its ability to observe nature in terms of its long-term quantitative trends of cause and effect. This is in stark contrast to the type of natural selection characterized above as "old science." The modern view of nature is mostly afforded by the use of computers that can deal with huge amounts of data, and has been paramount in allowing science to model ecosystems and track the implications of human impacts on the biosphere. Computer modeling of nature is a very effective inductive method for describing the long-term common behavior of large systems, but it also leads us on a path that becomes blind to all those little events that significantly influenced the ultimate outcome, and usually completely discounts the unique events that were contrary to the trend. Modern science is therefore in some ways the opposite of old science, because it increases our focus on common knowledge and glosses over the unique and fantastic.

This book is a collection of some of those choice unique events that are the more traditional fodder of natural history. These are real stories about people's experiences with our counterparts in the ocean, the whales; beings we have only recently begun to interact with regularly on a non-predatory basis. As a scientist attempting to understand the thought processes of whales relative to our own, I have found the unique, non-repeatable and fantastic events to often be the most enlightening. As the late Gregory Bateson put it, "it is the difference that makes the difference."

"Greeting ceremonies" among the Vancouver Island Southern Resident Community of orca pods are an excellent example of a rare, enlightening behavior that for the average person would only be a once-in-a-lifetime experience. Greeting ceremonies are when the southern residents line up abreast as separate pods facing each other hovering at the surface, and then swim into each other, "intermingling" with members from the other pods. It appears to be a unique cultural tradition of this community of pods, just like rubbing in the gravel beaches of Robson Bight is a unique cultural tradition of the "northern residents."

As of this writing, 20 years of monitoring has produced some 15 greeting ceremonies that have been documented on either film or in detailed field notes. Originally it was thought that "greeting ceremonies" only happened when pods reunited after they had been separated for extended periods of time. Now, as a result of noting unique onetime variations, we know that sometimes these ceremonies also occur: a) when pods are about to separate after being together for long periods of time, b) at the end of multi-pod sleep sessions, and c) in the context of terminal illness in a pod member.

Other examples of extremely enlightening anecdotes about these orcas include the 1987 three week fad of pushing around dead salmon at the surface for hours at a time. It was a game that started in K-Pod and within a week had spread to all three pods. Or the kelp game that a colleague and I once observed, in which juveniles were pulling free-floating kelp bladders deep underwater and letting them go so they would break the surface like little missiles erupting from the sea.

However, of all the whale tales I have personally witnessed, the ones that stand out as the most amazing and enlightening are those short, one-on-one contacts with a wild whale; when the whale stops by the side of your boat and deliberately looks you in the eye. At that point the two of you have just shared a moment of time, each consciously focusing on the other, and in my experience it is always an adrenaline rush. You are short of breath, a little scared, and you feel like your soul has just been looked through. Those are the most personally enlightening whale encounters, but by modern standards, the scientifically least useful. Yet, are they scientifically irrelevant? If your goal as a scientist is to understand the thought processes of whales relative to our own, these complex games and rituals are very informative about the mind behind the melon. Each of the stories you are about to read tell us volumes about what interests whales, their sense of humor, and how remarkably similar our conscious experiences actually are.

As more and more people are exponentially added to the planet and our interest in cetaceans continues to grow, we will collectively have exponentially more whale tales to share. It is my hope that this book is just the beginning of the forum for sharing those experiences. If the whales have anything to teach us that is necessary for our survival, it will probably be in the sharing of these collective experiences and the retelling of tales colored by our personal insights from which the enlightenment will come.

Rich Osborne, resident scientist
The Whale Museum
Friday Harbor, Washington
September, 1995

The San Juan Islands and Orca Whales

Many of the stories in *Whale Tales*, especially the Orca Tales, take place in the San Juan Islands in Washington State. This archipelago of hundreds of islands is located between Vancouver Island and the mainland of North America. The islands stretch about 75 miles in a northwest-southeast direction. The more northern islands are in British Columbia, where they are known as the Gulf Islands.

These are the home waters of J, K and L pods of the southern resident orca whales. (A-I pods are the northern residents and are found in Alaska and northern British Columbia.) During the 1950s and 1960s approximately 45 of the southern resident whales were captured, or killed while being captured. Those kidnapped animals were put into aquatic prisons around America. An entire generation of orcas were removed from this population, which numbered 94 whales in late 1995.

Resident orca whales differ from transient orca whales in a number of ways:

- Diet: residents are primarily fish eaters; transients consume marine mammals, including the large whales, as well as anything else they come across that they want to eat.
- Vocabulary: about 50 different sounds have been recorded from residents; transients, less than 20 vocalizations. This makes sense as fish are less sensitive and aware of the orcas' presence than seals, sea lions and whales.
- Pod size: resident pods range from 18 to 50 animals; transients pods rarely are more than 6 or 7. Smaller hunting groups for more difficult to catch prey.
- Range: Both residents and transients have "home" areas where they are found. The southern residents range in an area with a 150 mile radius; the transients here range to about 600 miles away.
- Dorsal fin shape: The tip of resident's dorsal fins are much more rounded than the pointed dorsal fins found on transients.

These distinctions between resident and transient orca whales are found in these animals around the world.

Many minke whales are also found in the San Juan Islands during the summer.

There used to be a population of both gray and humpback whales here, but they were hunted out. Occasionally a humpback is spotted in the area.

In 1995, a record number of gray whale sightings were recorded, an indication of the remarkable recovery of this animal from near extinction, for the second time.

"You can't encounter a whale for the first time and not remember it for the rest of your life."

Dr. Roger Payne, who discovered that humpback whales sing songs

Whale Tales

Human Interactions
with Whales
volume one

Orca Tales

Here They Are!

Laurie Glenn lives on a small, outer island in the San Juans and is a dancer, tile setter, caregiver, and celebrant of life.

We were traveling back home on the "Puffin." There were three of us on the boat: Captain David, Carson, and myself. We were hauling a couple tons of food for the summer co-op order to the island. It was a beautiful early summer afternoon.

Feeling the magnificence of President's Channel, I had a thought which I expressed: "It has been a really long time since I've seen any whales. It sure would be nice to visit with them again." The others smiled and nodded silently in agreement.

You could not have counted to ten before the whales appeared in front of the boat. They were a quarter of a mile ahead of us, headed our way. David cut the engine and we drifted, watching them approach.

It was a young male and a young female killer whale. Three times they made passes by the boat, breaching three times on each pass. After their wonderful, showy display, they continued on their way and we on ours.

I felt happy and fortunate to be so subconsciously in tune with the whales. And I gave thanks that my little prayer was answered so quickly. ◁

Here They Are! II

Tom Averna runs a whale watch boat out of Deer Harbor on Orcas Island in the San Juan Islands. This story happened in the same channel as the previous tale.

From time to time on our whale watching boat, we experience days when there are no whales to be watched. Those days are much more difficult as we need to find other wildlife for our guests to see. The Islands are always here and beautiful to view, but it can sometimes be a challenge to find other things of interest. Eagles fly away, seals haul out on rocks we don't pass, porpoises play elsewhere, and who knows *where* the whales go.

Everyone aboard feels some disappointment when we don't get to see the whales.

We were just about back to Deer Harbor after a four-hour boat ride, during which we had seen no whales. Thaddeus Douglas, my sixteen-year-old first mate, was on the flying bridge with me. I was not feeling too happy when he told me, "I think we'll see some whales soon." I kiddingly told him to shut up or I was going to give him a hit.

As I mockingly raised my left arm and swung it back as if to hit his grinning face, I looked at the water behind him. There were the whales! He was right! They were swimming towards us! "Sometimes you just have to go with your feelings," Thaddeus said.

We stayed out an extra hour to enjoy the whales, while all the time Thaddeus stood there looking at me with an expression of amazement and wonder on his face. ◁

Watch This!

Emelia L. "Lee" Bave was instrumental in getting The Whale Museum established in 1979, on the top floor of the old IOOF Hall in Friday Harbor, Washington. She had restored the building from a condition best described as rotting away.

Lee used the ground floor of the building to present her play "Pig War Saga," an historical production about the confrontation which resulted in the San Juan Islands becoming American, rather than British, property. Since the 1950s Lee and her husband operated the Mar Vista Resort on San Juan Island.

Before there was any thought of making connections with whales, an incident happened to prove they do relate to humans. It is nice to know that through research and study, they aren't to be feared and are losing the name of killer whales and being better known as orcas!

In the early 1960s, before there had been anything done to bring attention to whales, I was sitting up on a large knoll by Crescent Beach at Mar Vista Resort on San Juan Island, enjoying the fabulous view. I could see in all directions; the mass of various varieties of wild flowers there had inspired me to write much poetry.

Then something occurred that took my mind off everything, and also drew the attention of several of our guests who were having a picnic and barbecue on the beach. A pod of at least ten orca whales were going down the Juan de Fuca Strait. When they got directly in line with the beach, the whales came close in and started circling and doing all sorts of lovely and tricky antics for us all to see.

They would circle, and weave in and out, and breach. But the most unbelievable action was when two of them would leave the group; all the people were standing on the beach, having forgotten all the food they were preparing. The two whales would spyhop and open their big mouths as they faced the people on the shore and nod their heads, as if to say, "Are you enjoying this?" Then the whales would nod some more, and hold their heads up, with their mouths still open, as if to say, "Watch this!"

They rejoined the other whales and carried on with all the things they were doing. They were there off the beach for at least half an hour.

I didn't have my camera with me, and videos weren't known at that time, or it would certainly have been a best seller. It surely would have let everyone know that orca whales do like to show off and relate to people! ◁

Get Back!

Van Gimlet received both California secondary and elementary teaching certificates. She found she preferred to work with younger kids, so she taught preschool for 20 years.

Van and her husband, Jim, reared their five children in southern California, but Jim had grown up on Puget Sound and they chose to retire there. She is glad they did: they both say the San Juan Islands are the best place they have ever lived.

I live on the southwest side of San Juan Island, in Washington State. We have an approximately 200-degree view of the Juan de Fuca and Haro Straits where orca pods swim between Cattle Point and Roche Harbor during summer months. I love watching these whales, and sometimes am fortunate enough to sight them several times a day, searching for food or playing.

All sightings are special to me, but two are most memorable.

In the summer of 1993, a baby whale was showing off for a crowd of people on a whale watching boat. He spyhopped and turned little back flips right next to the boat. His female caregiver, mother or older sibling, decided it was time for them to leave. She swam up to the youngster, nudged it, and started towards Cattle Point.

The baby followed for a bit, but then returned and continued to show off for the applauding people. The adult came back and nudged it again. Once more the baby followed only briefly, then swam back to play. This was repeated several more times to the delight of the people in the boat. At last the adult's perseverance prevailed; the show was over, and they swam on their way.

Another time, in the small bay below my home, there were two boats: a canoe and an inflatable life raft. The people in these boats seemed to me to be harassing the whales; getting closer and closer, not at all following the guidelines about maintaining a distance of one hundred yards from the whales.

Suddenly five orcas came up around the canoe and, in unison, as if doing synchronized swimming, they circled the canoe. The terrified people paddled for the shore fast!

Then the five whales encircled the life raft and repeated the display, spyhopping vertically around the raft. These people, also, headed for the shore, fast!

I had not realized whales would ever do that. Were they menacing, saying, "Look, guys, we've had enough!"? Or were they, too, showing off, as had the baby whale? I have no idea. But either way, I said, "Bravo, whales!" ⟨

Communication

Michael Baker *was born in Bremerton, Washington, and gradu-*
ated from Vashon Island High School in 1965. He has lived on
Orcas Island in the San Juans since 1980 with Rocky, his wife of 27
years, and their four children. He came to the Islands as staff engi-
neer for the telephone company, where he designed the fiber-
optic network that links many of the islands together. Michael is
presently a telecommunication consultant in fiber-optic system
planning and engineering. He's been working on the design of
the "information highway" around many major cities.

When he was a kid, many of Michael's family were commer-
cial fishermen. There were 52 boats in the family; uncles and cousins
and everybody had a fishing boat: 50 purse seiners and two troll-
ers. It wasn't a corporation; they all happened to be fishermen.
The family lived in Puget Sound and took off, more or less to-
gether, to southeastern Alaska every year, through the "inside"
waterway. There they saw lots of whales.

In recent years I've traveled around northern Puget Sound and
the San Juan Islands in a 14-foot fiberglass drift boat, a McKenzie
River dory. I was taking care of 19 different islands for the phone
company, so I traveled among them as often as I could in my dory.

One morning, I had a business meeting in Friday Harbor, on
San Juan Island. It was an easy walk from the dock, so I took
the dory over. Because there were visiting presidents and vice-
presidents of the corporation that owned the phone company,
it was a black-tie affair, and we all dressed up. The weather was
bad so I had rain gear over my suit and tie, unusual attire for
small boating.

The meeting went well and I left Friday Harbor about two
p.m., returning to Orcas. I like to go through Wasp Pass, so I
went north in San Juan Channel. I hadn't gone far, just past the
University of Washington's property, when I saw a pod of orca
whales coming south. They were out in mid-channel, so I turned
around to coast with them and throttled way back. I thought I'd
drift along in the same direction they were going and watch
them as they went past.

Suddenly, a huge male orca surfaced right beside me.

He came up so close that his dorsal fin was towering over the boat, and that was very startling for a first view of this whale! He had no more than done that when he went straight down and swam over so that his fin was in line with the center of my boat. I was looking ahead, and his head was a shadow way up in front of me and his tail was way behind; that 14-foot boat felt very little. He looked to be at least 30 feet long.

I immediately was awash with this feeling of fear because the whale was right there, under the dory. I was practically surrounded by him.

An instant after fear washed over me, a much more compelling consciousness washed over that with this very, very simple, basic thought-feeling: "Don't be afraid. Be observant. Watch my family."

Then it went away. They were emotions: don't fear, observe, family. It was so clearly communication that not only was I not afraid, at that moment I was in awe. Here I was, talking with my mind to this whale.

I remember that I was crying.

The orca would surface beside the dory and squeak a couple of squeaks and I would squeak back, trying to repeat what he was saying. It only lasted for a few minutes. At one point, I reached out for him because he was close enough to stroke his side. The whale's skin felt like a damp wetsuit.

I was reaching out and, since it was rainy, I had the rain gear on over my suit and tie. I was stretched out, petting the whale, so you could see the suit and tie. The dory was leaning over, and I looked up. As much as my little dory was leaning to the east, here came one of the state ferries towards us, over to the west.

Everyone on board was leaning over the rail taking pictures of me and this whale. I, of course, smiled as I stroked this big animal.

The whole thing was just too cool to believe.

There was no doubt in my mind that we had communicated. I felt he was holding back because he figured he would probably burn my brain cells out if we had more than fleeting images or concepts. I had this sense there was a really tremendous awareness there which had taken a moment to communicate to me to make sure I didn't get upset because of his presence.

If you've ever been in a dark room and wondered if someone were in it, you can often sense their presence even though they don't make a sound; there is something about being in the vicinity of another consciousness and energy.

It was very much from that part of my awareness that I felt the whale's consciousness. It was pretty remarkable. I felt very good about it, powerfully moved and quite calmed.

Even though I have literally seen hundreds of whales in my life, I had never before been close enough to any whale to feel its communication. I think because I had the outboard on and was in an area where there was much boat traffic that the whale was especially conscious and stayed with me while his family swam by. When they got completely past, with no ceremony, off he went.

This experience was like the "visions" that you read about. They don't happen very often in life, and when they do, it seems it is usually to other people. So it sticks with you strongly. Especially one of the good ones. I was in Vietnam for fourteen months, so I have had a number of bad ones. This one balances a whole lot of that, a whole lot of that. I delivered my own babies at home and that, also, balances the books real well.

We often have intellectual imaginings about life and what it can be. To have one such concept verified so strongly is pretty awesome. Most times the things that we intellectualize about are never things that we can verify or prove.

One just has to live with his or her faith.

In the question of whale consciousness and their vast intelligence, I don't need faith anymore.

I know for sure.

We have spoken. ✍

Pictures For Hyak

Kelley Balcomb-Bartok has been recognized as one of the premier photographers of orca whales. Kelley's career began at the age of thirteen when he accompanied his father, Ken, out in small boats, documenting the orcas of Washington state.

Ken began the Orca Survey in 1976 simply as a census of the orcas in the area. Now known as the Center For Whale Research, its efforts have grown into a full-fledged study of orca behaviors and social structures, as well as many other tangents.

Kelley has photographed and studied humpback whales in the Caribbean and the orcas in southeast Alaska, both before and after the devastating Exxon Valdez oil spill. He also was involved with the production of the Warner Brothers' movies Free Willy *and* Free Willy 2.

Kelley says, "Who would have thought, 20 years ago, that the public's interest would have grown this large, and that we would still be a part of it?"

Kelley is the person in the photograph on the cover of this volume of Whale Tales.

In 1987, John Ford, the marine mammal curator at the Vancouver, British Columbia, Aquarium, was working at his desk. There are three underwater viewing windows to the whale display tank in his office. A book entitled *Killer Whales* (which Ford, Mike Bigg, Graeme Ellis, and Ken Balcomb wrote and photographed) had fallen off the table down into the viewing window.

John noticed Hyak, one of the captive killer whales in the tank, gazing at the book. He told his friends and colleagues about this behavior, and eventually television crews came by to record Hyak looking at pictures.

I was intrigued by this behavior and began visiting Hyak in 1988. I became a regular visitor to the Aquarium: at least once, and often twice a month I would travel there and spend the entire day. I would bring stacks of images with me: my own drawings and photographs, as well as illustrations of killer whales in books, magazines and from other artists and photographers.

I carried the art work in a Haliburton case (a sturdy, aluminum camera case) with a big foot-and-a-half long killer whale sticker on it. The orca image was very visible. I would set the case in the window and Hyak could see this whale sticker from wherever he was in the tank.

Once he had spotted the case with its orca sticker, he would make a beeline for the window, wherever I was. I would then begin to show him the images I had brought that day.

I would have Hyak's complete attention: he was entranced by seeing those photographs and illustrations. The only stimulus for the whale was visual, images for his mind to contemplate. He had no other reward whatsoever for looking through the window at those things. This would go on for thirty to forty minutes, until Hyak got the signal from his trainers that the show was about to begin.

He would swim away to perform for the public with the other whales. At the end of the show, the whales swam in an "eschelon" formation three times around the tank. After their three loops, they were free to go where they wanted until the next show.

As soon as the show ended, you could see Hyak looking into the windows for where I was set up this time. Sometimes, I would begin to set up while the whales were still swimming in formation. Hyak would not break formation, but you could see him looking and registering where I was. When the three final loops were completed, he would swim directly to the window where he had seen me. It was clear that the whale was looking forward to coming over to see what I brought to show him.

I would lay out the materials I brought and begin to go through them. Perhaps I would begin with a photograph from *National Geographic*; he would look at it and either find it fascinating and study the image for up to two minutes, or not be interested in it at all. If he had no interest in the image, he would glance at it for less than one second, then raise his head and look me in the eye, until I put a new photo or illustration up to the glass. He would even study little two by three inches illustrations, if they interested him.

His eye was one inch away from the six-inch thick glass, and the illustration was pressed against the other side. We were very close to each other.

I would have him for thirty to forty minutes between the shows. He would stay submerged for five to six minutes, surface to take a breath, then drop right back down to the window to see what I would show him next.

Hyak had no interest in images of houses, airplanes, horses, cars, or trucks, things he could not relate to at all. But show him a salmon or other orcas, and he would study the picture minutely. It was a great deal of fun for me, as I was always trying to find new things to bring for him to see.

For a while, it was only Hyak who would come to see the pictures. After some time, Finna, the younger male orca, also showed a little bit of curiosity and would occasionally swim over and see what it was that Hyak was so interested in. Finna, however, would not stay very long.

The female orca in the tank, Bjossa, seemed to be annoyed that we would distract Hyak. On occasion, she would come over and just push him away. She would quickly look at what we were holding up to the glass, then swim on. Hyak would swim away while she was there, then come back to look some more.

It was interesting that word of all this got out. Sometimes when I arrived, there would be groups of school kids with their drawings of killer whales held up to the glass, with Hyak swimming from window to window looking at what they were showing him. The word spread and people would come with pictures to show Hyak.

Rather than only coming to see the whales, they would bring something for the whales to see.

He would go for it in the same way he went for what I showed him: if Hyak liked it he would study it in detail; if he did not like it, he would raise his head and look the person in the eye until they showed him something else.

He was especially interested in seeing killer whales. A spyhop was almost not enough to interest him, but if he could see most of the animal, he would be interested in it.

Some of the illustrations were a stipple technique; lots of dots which create an image. He would look closely at these images which had a lot of detail, so he could see the whale. He was completely into it.

I continued showing Hyak images until his death. Unfortunately, he passed away before we got to experiment very much with this. I had thought of graphically breaking up whale drawings, beginning with very simple black and white shapes and evolving through to what we recognize as the image of a killer whale. It would have been interesting to see at what point Hyak recognized and studied this series of images.

He was a very special whale. He was born a northern resident orca, and became trilingual by the time of his death in 1991. When Hyak was captured in 1968, the Vancouver Aquarium had a female orca from K-pod, one of the southern resident families. Over the years they were together in captivity before her death in 1980, Hyak learned many of the calls and vocalizations of K-pod. In 1981, the Aquarium brought in two Icelandic orca whales. Hyak learned many of these whales' calls as well, in their dialect.

It was sad what was done to Hyak's body after he died. I guess it was poor decision making on someone's part; I doubt if such a choice would be made today.

When the whale died, the people from the Vancouver Aquarium took his body out into the Strait of Georgia, and sank him. But he washed back up onto the shore. So they cut him up into pieces, hoping *they* would sink. But the pieces washed up also.

It was a pretty painful ending for a great whale and a friend. They could have gotten his skeleton and put it on display. But that was not the way they treated him. He had put his time in for twenty-three years; he died younger than he might have if he was not captured, and this is the thanks he got at that time.

As I said, I like to think that the body of the next killer whale that dies in captivity will be treated differently. ⬦

I'm a Boy!

Tom Faue moved to Canada in 1971. Born in Minneapolis, Minnesota, Tom spent two years in India and Africa. While on his travels, on the road to Kathmandu, the U.S. Federal Government wanted to send him to Vietnam. He had met all these Canadians who said, "Come to Vancouver! It never snows there, and it's the warmest place in Canada." So, Tom moved there.

He lived on a couple of islands, then ran into someone building a big trimaran. The boat builder was the local veterinarian, whom Tom met because his dog got into a fight and needed attention. Tom and the vet got to talking about boats, so they went into the backyard to see the huge trimaran the vet was building. They ended up designing Tom's boat together. The vet told Tom that a ten-year-old child could build one. Tom bought some tools and began to build his boat.

Launched in 1975, the boat has been Tom's home ever since. He has sailed her all over the British Columbia coast and has had a variety of jobs. Most recently, Tom has been working as a wood sculptor. He enjoys what he does and people have been supportive of his work. Tom is now doing more figurative sculpture and has used the following encounter to create a limited edition bronze orca which he believes portrays the majesty and power of this animal.

It was Thanksgiving weekend in 1989. We were coming back from Mayne Island and were between Saltspring and North Pender, at about one o'clock in the afternoon. We were traveling in my 38-foot catamaran, and it was a beautiful day.

All of a sudden I could see a killer whale's fin maybe a mile ahead, so I yelled to everybody. We kept motoring along, seeing how close we could get to it.

As we got closer we could see a smaller head in the water which we figured out was a seal. The killer whale was after the seal.

We turned off the motor and just coasted up to within a hundred feet of the whale. We could see the fin coming along the water, then submerge. All of a sudden the seal would pop out of the water with the whale coming up underneath it, nudging it. Then the seal would dive, and the whale would disappear. The seal's head would come up, and we would see the fin coming at it.

Sometimes the whale would breach out of the water and land on top of the seal. Then the seal would dive, and there would be nothing for us to see. The seal's head would surface, and fifty feet away here would come the fin towards it again. This went on for at least an hour.

There was just the one whale by himself. We weren't sure if the whale was male or female, yet. It so happened that the boat drifted right up to them, right next to the seal and the whale. We were all out on deck, four of us watching this show go on.

We thought that the whale would just go up to the seal and take a chomp out of it, and that would be all. Then we realized he was playing with it like a cat with a mouse.

At one point, the whale dove and came up under the seal with such force that both of them came out of the water, a full breach with a flying seal! We thought we got that on film, but we didn't. We got the whale in the air, but the seal is out of the picture. Still, it was a pretty amazing thing to see.

Again, the whale had the seal right next to the boat. By now it had gone on for almost two hours and the seal was so stunned that it wasn't moving much anymore.

We realized that he was going to eat the seal. He slowly submerged, seal in mouth, then surfaced again. It took him maybe ten minutes to eat it all. I thought it might have been gory and gruesome, but we didn't see much of that. He ate it mostly underwater.

So, that was pretty exciting. At the time we were a little scared, because we thought maybe if we got between him and the seal, the whale would feel threatened. We were a little worried about him smashing the boat; we didn't know what was going to happen next, but nothing happened to us.

We thought, well, that was going to be the end of it.

It wasn't.

After the whale ate the seal, he went absolutely crazy.

He put on this after-dinner show that went on for about another hour and a half. He swam away from the boat going full bore. He'd get about a hundred yards away, turn around and come straight for the boat like he was going to ram us. Just before he got to the boat the whale would dive underwater, then breach on the other side of us.

It was like this surge of energy after dinner got him all excited. All excited from the kill and who knows what.

The orca kept charging towards the boat and breaching. Then he came up right between the hulls where the bow net is, and looked up at us.

We were eye to eye out there.

We thought this whale must have escaped from an aquarium somewhere, because he was so friendly towards us and was putting on this great show. He was obviously performing and was totally aware that we were there. There were no other boats around. I brought out my flute and started playing it just to see what would happen. He went even more wild. Charging the boat, breaching out of the water, splashing the boat with his pectoral fin—this amazing display of attention towards us.

The whale had a fairly small dorsal fin, so we all agreed, "This must be a female." No sooner than had we said it must be a female than the whale came alongside the boat, five feet away again.

He turned over on his side and exposed himself to us, flashing us! Here is this great big "red sea snake" hanging there. We all cracked up laughing. It was as if he had heard our words or thoughts and wanted to make sure we knew that he was a male, not a female. It was pretty phenomenal timing, how that happened.

Then he had another burst of energy and swam away from the boat, charged it, submerged, and breached again and again.

The whole encounter lasted at least three hours. It was after four o'clock and we knew it was going to be dark in a couple hours, so we decided we had to get underway because we had miles to go. The wind had come up by this time, so we began to get the sails hooked up. As soon as we started not paying attention to the whale, and were working with the sails, that was it. The show was over.

That killer whale took off in a straight line away from us and disappeared. He knew that we were not paying attention to him anymore. We were convinced that he was putting on this show just for us, and was aware when our attention shifted, so he left us.

About two weeks later I was working on the dock, actually carving a killer whale out of juniper. A fellow came over and said, "Were you on the catamaran that was off North Pender Island a couple of weeks ago playing with the killer whale? My dad and I were on the shore watching the whole thing, and we couldn't believe it. It was just incredible."

Then, somebody said I should get in touch with the marine biologists up in Nanaimo. I can't remember how that exactly worked. But, one day Graeme Ellis came by and asked us to tell him the story.

We showed him the pictures and he explained to us that this was a transient, most likely, because they're the orcas that eat seals. He liked the pictures; they were good and the whale was right next to the boat. Often people show him pictures and there is a little bitty fin way in the distance.

Later, he got in touch to say that this particular animal was a whale that they knew, although I don't remember what number it had been given. He *is* a transient and has a reputation for wild behavior, like riding in the bow waves of boats.

Graeme Ellis had a theory about why the whale played with the seal for so long before he ate it. He thought it was because killer whales' eyes are so close to their mouths that the seal's flippers or tail could damage the whale's eyes if they get too close in their struggle. The whales stun the seals first before they eat them, so there is no danger of that happening.

It was an unforgettable several hours.⊲

Never As Good As The First Time

Jim Nahmens has been a naturalist and wildlife photographer since 1979. Each summer he leads trips to Alaska to see the humpback whales, glaciers and the Inside Passage wilderness. His tale takes place in British Columbia in 1989.

I was on a kayak trip around Johnstone Strait, near the northern end of Vancouver Island. Traveling with a group of eight, on the last full day of our week-long trip, we visited a place called Mamalilacula, an abandoned Native village.

We experienced strange and powerful feelings there: it gave us a sense of being connected with the natural world, as well as feeling harmony and grace.

After paddling fifteen miles that day, we were tired when we returned to our campsite. After dinner most of the group was ready for bed. David, our trip leader, asked, "Is anybody up for a midnight kayak tonight?" There was a beautiful moon, close to full.

Several of us who had the energy launched our kayaks and paddled out of the cove.

The bioluminescence all around us in the water was fantastic, phenomenal. Organisms glowed in green florescent sparkles, like fairy dust, swirling off the bows of our kayaks. Every paddle stroke made wonderful patterns in the surface of the sea. Drops of water falling off the paddles made bright, expanding rings, on the dark water.

There were no lights anywhere, only the moon which was beginning to set, glowing orange in the sky; and the anchor light of a lone sailboat in a distant cove. After half an hour the moon was gone, and the night became pitch dark. It was mid-August, the time of the Perseid meteor showers.

There we were, floating in our little boats, taking it all in.

The water was flat calm. It was warm, totally black, absolutely silent. This spectacular fireworks show of bioluminescence was going on in the water all around us; then the meteor shower started in the sky. The shooting stars were reflected on the water's surface like a mirror, in all kinds of colors, joining with the bioluminescence. I'm thinking, "What a wonderful day this has been. I'm lucky to be alive."

We began to paddle back to our camp. I was in a double kayak with Jonathan. We were a little less tired than everyone else so we kept getting ahead of the others. The leader would call to us to slow down, so we would stop and wait for the others to catch up, all the while enjoying the night.

I suddenly heard a clapping sound off in the distance. From my experience of being around whales, I said, "That sounds like a fluke slap."

We were joined by the others, and then we all heard the slapping sound again. We sat quietly listening for more sounds. After ten minutes we heard faint blows in the distance. We didn't know for sure what was making the noises; they could have been harbor porpoises, or Dall's porpoises, or even seals. Whatever it was, it sounded really interesting. We decided to go out in the darkness to the middle of Blackfish Sound. That way, if the animals were coming by, we would have a better chance to be near them.

We got out there and waited silently half an hour for them. It seemed like a very long time. We continued to enjoy the meteor shower and the bioluminescence.

Then we could hear them approaching.

The closer they got the more we realized that these were big animals, that they were probably orcas.

We counted the blows as each one surfaced: One, two, three...eight, nine, ten; too many to count. It sounded like an army of blows coming at us. The sound just kept on getting louder and louder.

It was very strange to be in a situation where you cannot use your eyes to see these animals; essentially, we were blind. All of a sudden we were mentally tripping on the fact that here were these whales coming our way and we had no chance of seeing them. We had to get used to using our ears to locate them and relating to them only in an auditory way.

Their approach took half an hour, so we had the time to become accustomed to listening rather than looking. The sound traveled far across the water and we kept thinking they were much closer than they actually were.

We estimated there must be 25 whales. A researcher with us was convinced that it was a "super pod." Now they were much closer. As they broke the surface to breathe, we could hear the water splash off their bodies. There was no way to see them, because it was pitch black. A few of the people were getting apprehensive, imagining the worst possible scenario: headlines reading, "Crazy nighttime kayakers attacked by killer whales!" Of course, it was too late now, we had nowhere to go. But we were right where we had chosen to be.

At last, suddenly, we were surrounded by orcas. Some passed us on the left, others on the right. Each time they surfaced with a loud "WOOSH!" sound, their exhalations were startling to us.

We actually did see two of the orcas that memorable night. One dorsal fin passed through the anchor light's reflection in the still water. The other orca was just a few yards from our kayak. We saw the bioluminescence in the water flowing off its dorsal fin and back as it came up and went down in the darkness.

The sounds that night were the most powerful aspect of the whole experience. Listening to the whales coming towards us, and actually hearing them separate to go around our group of kayaks, was amazing. We were literally surrounded by these orcas, but we knew that only from our ears, rather than our eyes.

What a wonderful experience!

Several years after this kayak trip I was at a marine mammal conference. I remembered the name of the researcher who was with us, and listened to a lecture she gave. After her talk, I went up to her and said, "You won't remember me, or my name, but I bet you'll remember this experience...."

I recalled it to her and her eyes widened before she said, "Oh, yeah, that was pretty incredible." It was *her* most powerful orca experience as well. ✒

Minke Tales

Coming Up!

Ed Seifert began scuba diving seriously in 1964, and has been around boats and the water ever since. He has a degree in chemistry, worked as a marine chemist, and learned to be an instrument technician, which led to a job as a scientific technician in oceanography at Oregon State University for 18 years, three years of which were spent at sea. He has installed instrument moorings all over the world's oceans, particularly in the high latitudes.

Semi-retired now, Ed continues to dive, primarily installing and servicing boat moorings.

The first time I used our boat after moving to the San Juan Islands, my wife and our daughter were with me. We were going past Whale Rocks at the southwest corner of Lopez Island. We were about a hundred feet away from the rocks, when suddenly the depth sounder showed the bottom coming up, and up, and up. It didn't make sense because I knew from having studied the chart closely that we were in deep water, and the depth sounder had never acted strangely before.

I pulled back on the throttle, then put the motor into neutral. Even when we had stopped, the "bottom" continued to come up. It made no sense until....

Right in front of us, twenty feet ahead, a whale blows at the surface, takes a breath and dives.

It was a minke whale. He had been right under the boat coming up and the depth sounder was bouncing off his back! That was the only time we saw the whale.

It was a unique and interesting introduction to boating and whales here. ⊲

Pleasant Surprise

Richard Martin *is a research scientist at the University of Washington Primate Center. He works with computer modeling of brain anatomy to try to provide a "map" for people to do their research. Some of his work has been adopted by the National Library of Medicine for their framework for neuroanatomy terminology. He says it sounds neat but is often dull and tedious.*

Initially, Richard was studying marine biology at the Marine Bi-Medical Institute in Galveston, Texas, where he did research on an electric fish called the "Stargazer" which has batteries of modified muscle tissue in its head. The fish electrocutes small fish and then comes out of the sand to eat them. Then Richard began working with monkey neurophysiology.

Richard has always missed, and has kept an interest in, the world of marine biology; he is also a sailor.

We had been in the San Juan and Gulf Islands in our sailboat, a 27-foot Morgan, for several weeks. We have seen orca whales a number of times and have had them spyhop right next to the boat and look down on us. But this particular trip we had not seen any whales.

A little storm came through the night before we were going to return home. My wife and I took turns standing anchor watch all night to make sure we knew if the anchor dragged. I got more sleep than she did, for some reason. Maybe I had decided that we had done all that we could, and that we really were safe.

The next day we came all the way to the Strait of Juan de Fuca and made our crossing to Port Townsend. That is always a little bit exciting in a small boat but this time it turned out to be quite a handful. Just out from San Juan Island we encountered a significant ocean swell and about 20 knots of wind, which we found very rough.

We paid our dues. It was like when Joseph Campbell talks about the hero going through a crisis in order to reach the other side. This was it quite literally. Eventually we got those ocean swells behind us, so that we were surfing down them. The weather cleared up and it was beautiful by the time we got to Port Townsend.

It was actually flat calm when we got in past Point Wilson and into Admiralty Inlet. We were motoring along at a couple of knots, relaxing and enjoying ourselves. Towards the shore by Fort Worden, I saw a type of whale I had only seen at a distance out in the Strait by Hein Bank, a minke.

We kept on our course, got the binoculars out and started watching the whale. Each time after he would sound, he came up closer to us. Eventually, he got right next to our sailboat. The whale was just about the same size and shape as the boat. He matched our speed; by this time we were going dead slow, motoring along at probably a quarter of a knot.

The whale started swimming upside down underneath the boat, six or eight feet from the hull. He would swing around and come up on the other side in front of the bow. Then he would swing around again, upside down. We could see his eye and the white spots on his belly, those big patches of white.

I had never seen a rorqual whale that close. When he was upside down, we could see the pleats in his throat. When he was right-side-up, his twin blowholes were clearly visible. As he swam under us, I took a lot of photographs of the whale.

At some point he drifted off a little behind us and a big boil of bubbles came up from underwater. Since the wind was now from aft of us, we got this really strong whiff of what smelled like tuna catfood. I think that must have been a whale belch. It was really impressive to sense something tangible from a whale, as usually it is only visual stimulation.

The whale stayed with us about twenty minutes playing around right beside the boat; then he started working his way away. We never changed our course. He went half a mile or so away while we maintained the same slow speed so we could watch him for as long as we could.

For the next fifteen minutes, we suspected he was feeding because he made a couple of deep dives. Then he swam back over to us, and escorted us another ten minutes or so.

Eventually he left.

It was very neat. I had no idea at that time that rorqual whales were curious like that. But I've read since then that one of the minke's downfalls is that they are quite curious, and that makes them easy for whalers to hunt. ✍

Opportunistic Feeding

Michael Kundu is the owner/principal of Arcturus Adventure Communication, an alliance of nature photojournalists dedicated to promoting ethical and symbiotic environmental stewardship. He left a job in Public Affairs with Atomic Energy of Canada for, as he says, "better quality of life." He is an active kayaker and rock climber.

I like to kayak in remote areas, and one of the most isolated places accessible by car in North America is in Eastern Quebec, near the confluence of the Saguenay and St. Lawrence Rivers. The Saguenay drainage covers about two thirds of Quebec. The water depth a few yards off shore is very deep; for example, near the hamlet of Bergeronnes the water is 200 fathoms deep. The marine life in this basin is amazing. There are tremendous amounts of nutrients in the water: krill, diatoms, and plankton. Many cetaceans come here to feed: fin, blue, beluga, minke, and orca whales, and several types of porpoise.

I've spent several vacations kayaking in these waters with whales feeding around the boat. One summer, with a friend's help, I videotaped my marriage proposal while in a kayak with whales in the background. I later surprised my girl friend with it after dinner at a very nice restaurant. As the waiter brought dessert, the maitre d' brought the video monitor. My love watched the taped proposal and, to my great happiness, she said, "Yes!"

The next year, kayaking in the same area, I had been out among a group of six or seven belugas and was on my way back to shore. I noticed a minke whale swimming towards me, so I stopped paddling.

The whale came within thirty feet and began to feed. It seemed to me that she was corralling baitfish which were feeding on an upwelling of nutrients, including krill, against the kayak. To test that theory, I quickly paddled a hundred feet away and stopped. The whale swam to where the kayak was and did the same thing again!

She was using my boat as a blockade to keep her food from leaving. I stayed in that spot half an hour and simply watched her eat.

The next day I went out again and the same minke swam to me and repeated that behavior. She would feed at the surface on krill and fish whose escape was blocked by my kayak. The whale had a distinctive "sickle"-shaped saddle patch. The second day I assisted her feeding for several hours, reveling in how close we were and appreciating her graceful swimming.

To me, the biggest value of this experience, like most wilderness related experiences, is that I shared a special, symbiotic experience with a creature still considered alien by our race. Today, I look at maps of the region and feel a sense of sadness that the St. Lawrence whales, "my" whales, are in peril from pollution and other anthropogenic impacts.

Mostly because of my meeting with her, I think about Sickle. Minke whales, which travel the span of the North Atlantic, are the target species of Norwegian whalers. I hope Sickle remains within coastal waters. It would be a great tragedy to me to think that her final meeting with humankind might be as the target of a cold, steel explosive harpoon from Norway. ⚓

Mid-Atlantic Gymnastics

Tom Averna is a marine surveyor, sailor, and owner of Deer Harbor Charters, on Orcas Island in Washington, where he operates a wildlife and whale watching business.

He lived aboard and cruised in the Caribbean for ten years, skippered several large schooners. Tom told the tale on page 3, "Here They Are! II."

One of my long-held sailing dreams had been to make an east-to-west crossing of the Atlantic Ocean.

That dream was realized in December, 1993, when I joined June and Tom Wharburton, and their son Barry, on their 42-foot Roberts' ketch, "Mirabar." We made the 2,900 mile passage from the Canary Islands to Antigua in 25 days. We sighted minke whales three times; two of those encounters were fantastic experiences.

The first whales we saw just passed us by. There was a fair breeze blowing; we were running wing and wing, sailing at about six knots. A pod of three minkes simply cruised past, virtually ignoring the boat.

That, however, is not what happened with the other four whales we saw.

We had sailed thirteen days, maybe 1,800 miles from the Canaries, and were about halfway across the Atlantic. It was a beautiful, clear sunny day: a very light wind was blowing at less than five knots. The sea was calm, with a low swell. The surface was glassy smooth and the visibility downwards into the blue water was terrific. It seemed you could look down forever, with streaks of sunlight going deep, deep into the ocean.

I was on watch, trying to keep us moving west, sailing at less than two knots. It was really peaceful. Simon and Garfunkel's *Greatest Hits* was playing on the tape deck. I heard a sound like a whale breathing behind us. I turned, and there were three minke whales swimming toward us. Unlike the others, these were not travelling past us. They were coming to check us out.

They were adults, about 25 feet long, swimming on the surface. They each circled the boat twice. Then, right alongside the boat, not more than five feet away, they began rolling over and over. It seemed as if they were moving in time with the music. One swam on each side of the boat, with the third whale under our keel, doing somersaults: nose down, tail up, end over end. The water was so clear you could see every single part of the whales. It was an amazing sight.

At one point, I was up on the bow hooting and hollering at the whales when they surfaced to breathe. The whale swimming under the keel dove straight down. He just went deeper and deeper; I could easily watch him in the clear water. He went so deep that the whale was just a tiny turquoise speck, with his white underbody reflecting light through the blue sea. I estimate that the whale was at least 150 feet deep.

Then, just as suddenly as he dove, he turned around and began to surface. The bright blue speck was getting larger, and larger. Ten feet under our bow, just below me, the minke did a forward upside-down roll. It was a wonderful thing to watch.

The three minkes played around our slowly sailing boat for 30 to 40 minutes. We were totally awed by their performances. We felt privileged to be able to view the underwater ballet produced just for us. They also seemed to be enjoying themselves as well.

Then the music ended. June went below to put on another tape and chose Mozart. As soon as the new music started the whales left us! They gathered together the way they were when we first sighted them and swam away. I don't know if they got tired of being with us; but, with apologies to classical music fans, it seemed to me it could have been the different beat of the music. I don't know why, but they were gone when the tape changed.

Our third encounter with a minke took place on the final day of the passage. We had just sighted Antiqua, about 40 miles away. The "Christmas Winds" were blowing on our stern, 25-30 knots.

We were flying along, just hauling butt. The swells were about 15 feet high and nicely spaced apart. It was some wild sailing, a great final day for a passage.

I was at the wheel and looked behind at an approaching swell. There was another minke, body surfing down the face of the wave! This one was a youngster, about 15 feet long.

He would surf down the swell right to the boat, then dive under the stern. He would swim under us and spyhop three or four boat lengths ahead and look right at us. Just before we were about to run into him, he would dive. We would lose sight of him for a short while, then, "Here he comes again!"

He would be behind us, doing it all over again.

He was playing with the boat, there is no question at all about it. He did the same thing over and over again, for about an hour and a half. This was also quite a performance, thrilling, spectacular and far beyond anything I could have imagined a minke whale ever doing. I wished that we had a video camera aboard so we could have recorded the outrageous behavior of this whale.

I was surprised at the way these minkes responded to our boat in the open ocean. From what I've seen of minkes around the San Juan Islands, I thought they were elusive and shy and do not interact with boats very often.

After the trip across the Atlantic I did more reading about minkes and learned that, in fact, they are very curious out at sea. And, they travel in the company of other whales of their own age and gender, often three or four at a time. In our inland waters they are mostly solitary.

I cannot help but wonder, and worry, if minke whales are as curious about a whaling ship as they are about a sailing ship. If they approached a boat that was hunting them the way they did us, they would be all too easy to kill.

I am bothered by that thought because Norway is currently hunting and killing minke whales, and Iceland wants to hunt them also. I worry about the fate of those whales which were so friendly and entertaining toward us while we were visitors in the part of this planet which is their home. ✍

Humpback Tales

A Smart Aleck Kid

Rosemary Clifford *is a Rhode Island homemaker who worked as a senior merchandise manager for J.C. Penney. When her second child was born, she quit her job to be at home with her family. Her husband continues to work for J.C. Penney.*

We were on a whale watching boat off Plymouth, Massachusetts. It was large, 100 feet long, with 80-90 passengers aboard.

We saw many whales, between 10 and 20 of them. There were several species: fin, minke and humpback whales. Some came up close to the boat, but one made a memorable impression on us.

One adolescent humpback whale came right alongside the boat.

Of course, we were watching his every move and taking pictures. He, or she, was about 20 feet long. He came to within six feet of the boat and stopped. Then, this young whale looked directly up at us and began to slap the water with his pectoral fin, getting us all wet!

He swam down the entire length of the boat doing the same thing; splashing everybody who was looking at him. I mean, his little eyeball was right up out of the water looking at us.

He knew what he was doing. It was intentional.

When he got to the stern of the boat, the whale turned around and swam along the length of the other side doing the same thing, splashing everyone with his pectoral fin.

It was amazing, and funny! I put my camera away at once and it did not get wet, but others' cameras got wet. Just about everyone on board was drenched by the whale. The splashing lasted about five minutes.

The whale was like a smart aleck, wise-guy kid playing a prank on us whale watchers; it was something to remember. ✒

What Was That!

Ki McKenzie is a freelance writer and sometimes hospice worker. Joseph Bettis, a retired professor of philosophy and religion, taught at Western Washington University in Bellingham. They live aboard "Sundown" in Friday Harbor, Washington.

We were in Appelton Cove in southeast Alaska, anchored for the night. We were on our way to Sitka aboard "Sundown," a former purse seine boat, 64 feet long. It was about one o'clock in the morning, and we were in bed asleep.

An incredibly loud noise against the hull of the boat, right alongside our bed, woke us up suddenly. It was a resonant bass note followed by a big explosion that sounded like bubbles hitting the side of the boat.

We both sat up, simultaneously, and said, "My God! What was that? What was that?" We ran around the boat trying to see if there was a big leak somewhere. We ran up above decks and looked out in the water: nothing, nothing.

It was calm and quiet in the cove.

"What was that? What could that have been?"

We went back to bed.

The noise happened over, and over, and over again.

For the better part of 45 minutes to an hour, we could hear it move off, away from the boat. Then this amazing noise would come back and be right against the hull again. It was always a resonant bass note: a deep, vibrating bass note, and then a huge explosion that sounded like a water hose hitting the side of the boat. There was the sound of an explosion of bubbles against the side of the boat.

Joseph's first thought was that it was a whale. But it seemed unlikely to us that a whale would be in this small protected cove. In talking to people later about our experience that night, we learned that humpback whales will occasionally come into very small bays. In describing the noise, someone said that it did sound like humpback behavior. The bay we were in was just off Chatham Straits, where there are large numbers of humpback whales.

It surprised me, because the bay we were in was well off the open waters. It was back in around a couple of corners; a shallow, flat cove without a lot of sea life in it. It wouldn't have taken much for it to have been a slough.

We never saw the whale, we only heard it; but we heard it really well.

We did not get much sleep that night. ✍

Life Story

Richard L. Wallace is an academic, a professional, and a scientist. But he is first an environmentalist and nature lover, having inherited his father's love for nature and the outdoors. He says has been blessed with mentors at every academic level who have supported his ambitions, goals, and dreams.

When I was 12 years old I went on my first whale watching trip, out of Provincetown, Massachusetts, on a beautiful July day. It was sunny with fairly calm seas.

I had never seen a whale before, other than a couple of belugas at the New York Aquarium, in Brooklyn. I was very excited to see humpback whales; this was in the early 1980s and that was what was usually seen on a whale watching trip in the Southern Gulf of Maine.

In a very short time, we saw a number of humpback whales and, prominently, a mother and her calf, which was very exciting for me. We followed them around for a little bit at a distance. The calf was an unidentified animal that had been born that year or the year before, if I remember correctly. I was at the very front of the boat, on the bowsprit, and the calf dove. The mother remained on the surface.

I was looking around for where the calf would come up. As I looked down under the bowsprit, the young whale surfaced directly below me. The whale spyhopped out of the water nose first, then slanted to the side, looking up at me with its left eye.

The image is burned into my memory.

At that moment I was looking over the rail into the eye of a humpback whale, which was probably relatively equal to myself in maturity. We held eye contact for what seemed like an eternity to me, but was probably all of about ten seconds, before the whale slowly sank back into the water. It dove, then surfaced again with its mother.

That moment inspired me, that connection which I made with the young whale, the visual connection, looking down into the eye of this whale that was near in its life to where I was in my life at that time. It motivated me to pursue a field of interest, study, work, and a love which I have continued to this day.

The year after this encounter, I volunteered at the New York Aquarium working with their beluga whales, the very first whales I had seen. The next summer I attended the School For Field Studies' humpback whale Ecology Program in the Bay of Maine. I went on to major in Environmental Studies as an undergraduate at the University of Vermont. My thesis was on the conservation of humpback whales in the Western Atlantic, focusing on programs in the Dominican Republic and the United States. I earned my Master's at Yale where I studied protected species policy and marine mammal conservation.

I then worked for the Marine Mammal Commission in Washington, DC. This is a small Federal agency which advises other government agencies involved in marine mammal protection. I have since returned to Yale where I am now working on my PhD, studying decision-making in federal agencies and using marine mammal recovery programs as my case studies.

I basically credit the experience between myself and that humpback whale calf as being the start of my life with marine mammals. It has sprouted into a productive career which I hope will last for many years.

Although I cannot provide for others the experience that I had with that humpback calf, I hope to pass on to my students an understanding of and desire to experience the realm of possibilities and rewards which can be found in nature, especially in the oceans. Perhaps, they too will find inspiration similar to mine. Eventually I plan to teach and hope to instill in my students a concern for, an affection for, and a desire to learn more about wildlife, and the care with which we must protect, conserve, and manage biological diversity. ⬐

Positive Energy Karma

Jennifer Durnin *has been a marine videographer in Hawaii since 1990. She also serves as a naturalist on a diving boat for a non-profit organization, helping educate divers about coral reefs, reef dwellers, and marine mammals.*

This is not just a story of me alone. It involves thirteen other people.

We were on a charter boat, a 53-foot catamaran, traveling between Maui and Lanai, when we spotted a humpback whale. We thought, at first, that it was a mother and her calf about 150 yards away. The captain of our boat, Jeff, does a whale talk on the trip every day, so he decided to stop the boat at that point and tell a little bit about the whales. Ten minutes later, the whale started swimming towards our boat. We could see then that it was a solitary whale. She did a spyhop about fifteen feet off our stern, and stayed with us for about two hours.

The whale would roll over onto her back then rightside up, again and again. She continually positioned herself beside our boat so that we could pet her rostrum. I was able to record all of this on video.

We estimated the whale to be only four or five years old.

She was the most curious whale I've ever met in my life. She stayed, literally, right next to our boat for two hours.

Every single person aboard petted the whale—it was kind of like a game to her. The first half hour, while she was just looking at us, we were screaming, "We love you! We love you! You are beautiful!"

I think she really picked up on our energy and our noises and was very curious about us. Because the whale came so close to the boat, Jeff leaned over the side to see if he could touch her. When he did, she must have realized that's what we were trying to do. She spent the rest of the two hours positioning herself all around the boat close enough so that we could all get to pet her.

Everyone aboard touched this whale.

In four years as a naturalist whale watching here, I'd never had this experience before. A lot of the researchers in Hawaii who heard about it saw the video and said they were amazed at her behavior—she was just so curious and interested in being with people who put out positive energy to her.

After the whale left our boat, she went to another boat and came close to them as well. It was a bigger boat and the people were much more quiet and restrained. I guess that boat's naturalist did not encourage the people to make noise. The whale only stayed near them for half an hour.

We had been telling the whale how much we loved her and how beautiful she was. We were all talking to her, just giving the whale our "love" energy. I know this sounds kind of funny, but we were all so excited and positive about her being so close to us that I think she picked up on our feelings.

The video I made of the encounter with this curious humpback whale really shows that she wanted to be with us.

At one point, the other crew member held me by my ankles, upside down in the water, so I could get some underwater shots. (It's illegal here to go swimming with the whales.) The whale literally came right towards my camera, closer and closer. She rolled over onto her back and came up vertically below me, within five feet of the camera lens. The whale looked directly into it with her right eye. Then she rolled over and winked her left eye at me! I thought she waved her pectoral fins at me as she swam away.

It was really spectacular. This whale was simply the most graceful animal I've ever seen in my life. ⋞

Gray Whale Tales

The Whale Rug

Lisa Lamb got her captain's license in 1987. She enjoys taking people out on charter looking for wildlife and whales in her un-inspected vessel, a hydrofoil boat built in Russia.

She and her husband Neil live on an out island in the San Juans. They find it quieter than the main islands which are state ferry served. Although very boat dependent, she almost never uses a car. Lisa says, "I feel lucky to live where I do and do what I do at this time in the world's life."

We used to live on an old 96-foot wooden boat that had been very much vandalized, trashed, sunk, and everything else. We were fixing it up in Liberty Bay, by Poulsbo, Washington, out at anchor. There was a long, narrow runner of a rug in the boat that was filthy. The only way I was ever going to get it clean was to hang it overboard in the water on a rope. So I did that. Just threw it over, swished it around, and let it soak.

The rug had been over the side a few hours when there was this little "puhw" sound right next to the boat. We looked in the water, and there was a juvenile gray whale.

Well, a young gray whale is about twenty-five feet long, but it was still not as big as it could be. He hung out at the boat for two days, right around the boat. He seemed to really like that carpet. It was interesting because he would come up right next to the boat, and I was able to see that he had problems with his blow-hole. He had what looked like an infection around his blowhole. He also seemed to be spending an inordinate amount of time on the surface.

The whale was scratching and rubbing up against the rug, and appeared to us to be having a good time just hanging around the big boat, which probably reminded him of his mother. We kept wondering where his mother was.

Then the whale went over by the Poulsbo marina. All these other people in boats discovered him, and kind of chased or fol-lowed him for a while. The whale ended up swimming down to Dyes Inlet. He beached himself near Silverdale and died.

We got really bummed out about that, so we decided to leave Poulsbo, and pulled up our anchor. We went out Agate Pass, through Port Madison and around to Port Gamble, which is going into Hood Canal. It's got a tiny little "hurricane hole" where you can stay and not get any weather, so we anchored out there. I had pulled the rug up and washed it a little bit before we left Poulsbo,

but it still wasn't very clean. The rug was in the way and it was all wet. So I hung it back overboard.

There we were.

Now, all this time we had this great big white dog, a Great Pyrenees, on the boat with us. Saint Bernard dogs, by the way, come from the combination of a Mastiff and a Great Pyrenees.

This dog was out on deck. I was doing some stuff in the cabin, and Neil was working in the engine room. We heard my dog do a very strange bark, not your normal Great Pyrenees roar. It was like a, "Rrroooeeeiiifff?" We ran out there to see why the dog was making that very unusual noise. There was my dog almost over the side of the boat standing on the rub rail, with all four toes ready to leap in the water.

There was a huge gray whale right next to the boat. Same deal, nosing around that old rug. Only this time, it was *mom*. This whale was 45-50 feet long.

We got the dog back on the boat, more or less. We didn't let him jump over and attack the whale. This big whale was swimming around the boat in much more of a threatening manner.

The dog hadn't acted like that around the baby at all. He didn't mind the baby coming around and rubbing up against the boat, but, boy, that mom was doing too much thrashing and moving fast and really sniffing around. It seemed like she was really sniffing around.

The baby had rubbed up against that rug; I think there was scent in it or something. I've never been able to get confirmation that they can actually smell underwater, or maybe it was taste. In any case, the dog was quite concerned, and let us know it.

The whale went away after a while, up the bay into the mudflat. She looked around in there for a while.

We watched to see where the big whale would surface. Then she swam away. ⋘

Back Seat In A Kayak

Janet Mock was an environmental health specialist for the King County Health Department in Seattle. She now teaches, after devoting four years to becoming a serious amateur naturalist. This story is continued in the next tale, "Front Seat In A Kayak."

I was out in a double kayak with my friend Chris Harmon in Chuckanut Bay, just south of Bellingham, Washington. We put in at Larabee State Park and paddled up to the bay.

We were having a great time looking around.

"Jan, I think I've seen a whale!" she cried.

"No," I replied, "You've probably just seen a big seal."

We paddled a little more. "Jan, I really think I saw a whale!"

Again I told her, "No, you haven't seen a whale, you might have seen a sea lion." I did not believe that a whale would be in this small bay. And then a gray whale came up about twenty feet from the kayak and exhaled.

It was obvious to me now. Chris, in the front seat of the kayak, had seen a whale!

We watched it roll and go down. We were a little bit scared, and backpaddled so the kayak was closer to the clifflike shore. We sat, paralyzed by fear at first, and then watched it with great wonder. For ten minutes this gray whale swam around in Chuckanut Bay, often surfacing very near our kayak. Then he moved off.

We were sure it was a gray whale. It had barnacles and was the right size and everything.

It was between Dot Island and the south end of the bay. ✑

Front Seat In A Kayak

Chris Harmon works as a bookkeeper for a dentist; she is also a mother and a wife. Her family has lived in Bellingham, Washington since 1978, and they are really passionate about being on the water.

This is the same kayak as the previous tale.

Jan and I had gone out for a "Girl's Day Kayak." We were both real novices at it, especially me. I had been in bigger boats often, but never in one of these small, narrow kayaks.

We were just chatting and blabbing, having a good time and paddling along the shoreline, very much enjoying a perfect day. As we paddled into Chuckanut Bay, I was looking out over the water from the front position in the kayak. It was so pretty, the water was flat calm. The sensation of being so close to the water was growing on me, but it was so new I was not totally at ease.

All of a sudden, not far in front of us, I saw a little bit of wave action. It looked like a rock which was exposing itself, and the wave went up and down.

Then, this water spray shot out of the rock!

I said, "Jan, there's a whale!" Stories of Jonah and the Whale and all types of things rushed through my mind. I felt really, really small in the kayak.

At first, Jan didn't believe me, because I was the only one who could see the whale. I saw him again, right in front of us. Then he surfaced more to the side, and Jan knew it really was a whale. We immediately backpaddled to hug the shore as close as we could. We got a little fearful that he might get too near and come up underneath the kayak.

We watched him surface and become interested in us for a short time. Then he swam away. It was really an incredible experience to see a whale all alone from a very small boat. We've been out in boats a lot and it's neat to see whales, but you're usually with a zillion other boats. This was so private for Jan and me. The whale obviously knew we were there and did not seem to mind our watching him as he surfaced, dove, and swam around.

We found out later that the whale, a young gray whale, was sick and that he died soon after. We were concerned about him, because they are usually not seen here, so we called the Whale Hotline and made them aware that he was here.

It was really special. When I think about great experiences in my life, that's number one on the list of things I remember best. ✐

(Chris grew up on nearby Whidbey Island, so whales were a part of her upbringing. She lived by Penn Cove. When she was in grade school in 1970, a group of businessmen and fishermen cap-

tured and corralled a pod of the local orca whales. *Four of the whales were killed in the capture and seven others were taken away and put in prison—on display in relatively tiny tanks, and trained to do tricks for the paying public who continue to flock to see such shows. Chris was among a group of grade school children who were picketing in protest of this capture. Tokitae ("Lolita") was one of the whales captured at that time*

The orcas no longer enter Penn Cove, or any of the other locations where they were captured and their family members taken prisoner. In August, 1994, a collection of previously unseen photographs from the Penn Cove capture were donated to the Center for Whale Research on San Juan Island. Many of the orcas which had been captured and released were identified as still being alive.- pjf)

Baby Gray Whale In Our Gill Net

V. A. Luckhurst *is from Dillingham, Alaska, and has fished in Alaskan waters much of his life. He also tells the story on page 77.*

A friend of mine and I were fishing outside of Egegek, Alaska, and we caught a gray whale, a baby, in the net.

We were in a 32-foot long gill net boat, and the whale was small, probably 16-18 feet. We pulled up on the net, bringing it into the boat until we reached the whale. We tapped on the boat and talked to the whale and got it to calm down.

"Take it easy, we're gonna roll you out of the net. Just take it easy, everything is going to be all right." We kept pulling on the net, slapping on the boat and talking to the whale like it was a big dog.

That was kind of neat; when we talked to the whale, it relaxed. And when we slapped on the boat it relaxed.

The baby was probably in the net for fifteen minutes by the time we got it out. As soon as we saw it go in the net, we picked it (brought the net into the boat), picked back to the whale so it wouldn't tear the net up and hurt itself.

It was pretty amazing: the whale acted like it was cooperating because it quit thrashing about. We just rolled it back and forth in the net and rolled it right out.

It swam out, but then the mama whale came in there and started coming into the net. So we started slapping the boat again and pulling on the cork line, telling her to stay out of the net. She circled back around, then came over again.

The baby went out around the net, and the mama came back in. She was probably about 50 feet off the stern of the boat when she went up on her tail (spyhopped) and looked at us and wiggled her big eye. She just kind of looked at us and eyeballed us, then went back down and they both swam away.

Not very often do whales get caught in nets up there. That was the first time I ever saw a gray whale caught in the net.

Both whales swam away, and we caught a lot of salmon. ⬧

Friendly And Not So Friendly

Carol Miller *makes canvas products: boat covers and things like that. Her husband is an engineer who works for a food company.*

For four years they went to San Ignacio Lagoon, in Baja California, as part of a research program at the Orange Coast College. Through photographically documenting the whales, they were able to identify individuals who returned to the same area each year. They also recognize which calves were born to which mothers.

The Mexican government now allows only licensed Mexican boats to go out into the Lagoon with the whales now.

Carol's photograph from this tale is on the back of this book.

I'm not sure which story to tell, because we've had so many encounters with whales.

I suppose the best one is when we were in little Avon rafts. This was in San Ignacio Lagoon, in Baja California. There were four of us in the boat: two photographers, a driver, and an audio recorder.

A gray whale came to us and lifted up our boat.

When it picked up our bow, I wasn't sure what was happening. This was my first trip out. The bow just rose up, and I cried,

"Oh, my God!" I looked over the bow, and saw a 45-foot long animal below our 12-foot boat. The whale picked us up and moved us around with his nose, the front of his head.

He didn't move us far, maybe eight or ten feet. He didn't tip the boat at all; he just lifted it like we would have been lifted on a wave. Except there was no wave.

It was great.

Then he gently let us down. We just dropped our cameras to the bottom of the boat. We were hanging over the sides, holding on for dear life, watching the whale swim while keeping the boat in the air.

After he lowered us, we found that by rubbing the side of the boat, making it squeak, the whale would surface next to us. He would let us touch his nose and pet him. Then the whale swam around us a lot, so we got the cameras out and started filming.

We also had walkie-talkies but we were so excited we didn't call the other boats to tell them what was happening so that they could get there to experience a friendly whale. It was too thrilling to think of using the radio.

In the same lagoon, we also had an encounter with an un-friendly gray whale. We found what we thought was a feeding area for them. It was a relatively shallow area. The whales kept spyhopping. They had their mouths open with eel grass hanging out of them: eel grass in their baleen. We were photographing this because we thought it was interesting behavior.

Then one whale came by and charged at us. We thought, "Well, maybe he's going to be friendly." He swam around the bow, then came back and charged again across the stern.

I thought, "Oh, this is going to be neat. I think I'll photograph this one, because I'm going to get water coming off that tail fluke."

As the whale swam by our boat, he dumped water into the boat with his fluke! He sprayed us and we thought, "Oh well, he's testing us here."

He came back again and went under the boat, swam away— then came back at a full charge.

This time he was serious.

He came within inches of our outboard and lifted his fluke. You could see the handwriting on the wall here. I got my camera out of the way, because he really did a job dumping water on us on that pass.

We decided we had better get out of the area because he obviously did not want us there. He was filling the raft with water. We worried that maybe next time he would hit us broadside and dump us. This was not fun anymore.

We only had a little six-horsepower outboard, so we were not really speeding away, but we were leaving. The whale stayed with us, following us, until we were well clear of that area. Then he went back to the other whales. Whatever they were doing there was something they did not want humans to be witnessing.

There was another boat in the area at that time, and they experienced unfriendly behavior also. Their whale came up under their boat with such force that it broke the floorboards. They did not get dumped into the water, but they thought they would be. It was interesting, though scary.

We never learned why the whales were so protective of that area. Perhaps there were females giving birth. 🐋

Very Sensitive

Bruce Leavitt was born on Peaks Island, off the coast of Maine. His mother lived on that island for most of her life, traveling back and forth in a small boat in fair weather and foul, even when carrying Bruce before he was born. Perhaps this is the reason he has never been seasick.

Bruce's grandfather was a fisherman and taught him quite a bit about the sea. As he grew older Bruce developed a strong passion for boats and the water: he became a fishing guide/captain, served in the Navy, worked on a Sheriff's Patrol Boat in California, and for twelve years was a commercial fisherman, trolling for salmon and crabbing. He now volunteers with the Power Squadron in the San Francisco Bay area. Bruce has seen a lot of whales.

It's pretty well known that whales use an echo sounding technique to detect objects in their environment. Whales emit high frequency sounds; from the time and direction of the reflected sounds they receive, they are able to determine the location of food, obstructions, each other, boats, and so on.

Having spent many years at sea, I have enjoyed the company of whales on numerous occasions. I never knew just how sensitive the whales' sonar was, however, until I had a very close encounter with a pod of gray whales while commercial fishing several miles off the northern California coast a few years ago.

I will describe the circumstances of my close encounter by explaining how commercial salmon trolling is accomplished, so you will understand what the whales swam through.

Extending at right angles from the hull of the fishing vessel, on each side at a forty-five degree angle, are poles, the length of which usually depends on the boat's size. They are often as long as the boat, thirty to forty-five feet. From each of these poles are suspended up to six thin stainless steel cables weighted with lead cannonballs weighing up to sixty pounds. These weights keep the cables close to vertical underwater while the boat is traveling two to three knots.

The fisherman attaches floats to several of the cables, which shear the cables away from the boat, providing separation and preventing entanglement of the gear. On the cables at intervals are spreads (sports fishermen call them leaders) about twenty feet long. At the end of each spread is a baited hook or lure.

When I am trolling on my vessel, the "Sandpiper," I suspend stabilizers from the poles about six feet out from the hull at a depth of fifteen feet to minimize the boat's rolling. The distance from the stabilizers to the inboard cable is also about six feet. The combined total distance from one side of the farthest cable to the other is about eighty feet. The fisherman is combing the ocean for hungry salmon.

One beautiful July day, out about fifty miles southwest of San Francisco, I was having a good day: the fishing had been active. Since the autopilot was steering, I frequently checked that my course would not interfere with other fishing boats, or them with me. Many trollers, like myself, work single-handed.

On one such check I noticed another troller on a parallel course to mine, only headed in the opposite direction, about a quarter of a mile away. Then I observed a pod of gray whales between the other boat and mine. The whales were swimming in the same direction as the other boat. As I continued to work, I lost sight of the whales.

I kept on the same course, as I was having a productive day with lots of fish. I noticed that the whales had changed direction and were now coming toward me from astern. They were moving faster than my boat, so I figured that they would change course again to avoid the spread of wires around my boat.

Wrong! To my surprise they continued swimming towards me. I became concerned that they would entangle my gear, with possible dire consequences for me.

There was no way to get out of their path or bring my cables in.

I did not see any way that the whales would miss the spread of gear my boat was towing in their path.

As I held my breath, I saw a large male whale passing between the boat's hull and the starboard stabilizer, and a slightly smaller female just outside of him between the stabilizer and the inboard cable. On the other side of the boat, another female passed between the port stabilizer and the inboard cable, and just outside of her was a calf. I was surrounded by whales, all near the surface.

Not a single cable was touched!

Apparently the whales sensed the location of the underwater gear, and even as close as they came, there was no contact. As my breath returned, I saw them proceeding ahead of me, swimming toward Mexico.

Soon they were out of sight and I continued fishing, very much in awe of these whales' sensitivity at avoiding things in the water. ✒

You May Be Important, But That Was Goofy

Clyde Rice grew up on boats with his family. He has commercially fished and operated boats for The Scripps Oceanographic Institute for many years. He says that he realized he could not be out at sea all the time and maintain his marriage. So, he became a landscape architect and worked into being superintendent of parks for a small city. His wife's idea of getting out of the rat race was for them to operate a bed and breakfast on a big boat in Friday Harbor, Washington. Clyde was very happy to go along with that.

This story has to do with gray whales in the early 1950s. Dr. Paul Dudley White was a famous heart specialist; in fact, he was President Eisenhower's heart doctor.

Well, Dudley White wanted to take the heartbeat of a whale. He had all this fancy, expensive instrumentation and whatnot.

Julie Gomez '95

His idea was to shoot an arrow into a whale with these instruments attached to the arrow. Then he would be able to record the whale's heartbeat. We took him into Scammon's Lagoon in Baja, Mexico where there are a lot of gray whales. We had a small boat, a little wooden boat tuna tender, loaded with all his gear and this bow and arrow with which he was going to shoot the whale.

He wanted me to pull up alongside of a whale so he could shoot it. Then we would chase along with it while he got its heartbeat. Unfortunately, he didn't know about flukes coming down and smashing whale boats. More unfortunately, he didn't want to listen to what we tried to tell him about the historic behavior of these big animals when they were attacked by people in small boats. Gray whales were called "devilfish" by the whalers who hunted them, with good reason.

This was no whale boat, but we were doing the same damn thing. We were going to disturb this whale...quite a bit.

But Dudley White was paying the bills, and he urged me to get in close, right behind the forward fins. He took a shot with his bow and arrow.

Sure enough, just as I had tried to explain to him; the whale's tail fluke came down and we got smashed to pieces. Thousands and thousands of dollars worth of gear went down to the bottom. We had to swim to shore and leave the wreckage of our boat drifting around in the lagoon.

Then, we had to walk across the sand dunes and stand there on the beach for several hours waving and hollering, until they saw us from the ship and came to rescue us.

Dudley White later got a gray whale's heartbeat successfully— from a helicopter. ◁

Sperm Whale Tale

Midnight Snack

Michelle and **Kevin Marsden** live in the Gulf Islands of British Columbia. They have been actively sailing since 1979. They also contributed the story on page 65, "At Last!"

It was a really dark night.

A few stars were out, but there was no moon.

It was about one in the morning.

We were 1200 miles north of Oahu, sailing home to British Columbia from Hawaii on our 50-foot schooner.

On this particular night, there was a strange feeling that powerful events were taking place near us but we had no idea what. It just felt that way to both of us.

I was at the helm. Our windvane had packed it in several days earlier, so Kevin and I were taking wheel watches: four hours on, and four hours off. Of course, you get overtired and your mind starts playing tricks on you. We had probably put in 5,000 miles of ocean sailing in the previous three months.

It had never dawned on me before: you know you are out in the middle of the ocean and who knows what creatures are in the water under you? Until that night, I had never felt uncomfortable at the wheel.

That night I felt like I was being watched.

It was spooky.

For two nights we had been hearing the spouting of whales. You can often tell what kind of whale it is by the character of their exhalings. We looked it up and figured out that these had to be sperm whales around us, while other resource material suggested we were in that area where they traverse or feed. And, the books said that sperm whales' main source of food is the giant squid. Even though I had heard that earlier in my life, I always felt it was something out of Jules Verne.

That night we were sailing slowly, between three and five knots, just ghosting along. There was a lot of kafuffle and splashing going on all around us throughout the night. We were not sure if it was just waves or more than that. We never imagined that what was going on might be whales having a big feed of giant squid.

Being at the wheel in the dark of the night and realizing that around you it was pretty darned quiet except for those noises, you just didn't have any real idea of what was going on underneath the boat, 20 or 30 feet down. It was a very strange feeling to know that something *was* going on, but what?

It was quite an eerie thing the next morning: we were by ourselves in the middle of nowhere, after a long night of spooky, noisy activity in the darkness around us.

We were always on the lookout for glass balls and other interesting things floating in the water, so I had the net ready to pick up what we thought could be a glass ball in the water ahead of us. Kevin was up at the bow, I was at the stern.

He called, "You don't want to pick this up!" He could see ahead better than I could. What I saw was too brightly colored to be a glass ball. It looked like flesh, pinky-white.

I thought, "Oh, oh, it's something dead."

My imagination went wild: dead body, dead fish, dead something. When we went by it, there was the biggest piece of seafood I have ever seen in my life. It was a part of the main body of a giant squid. It was about three feet long and more than a foot wide, six inches thick. It looked like a giant piece of Dungeness crab. We took a photograph of it, but unfortunately, there is no point of reference to show the size.

We passed it by in amazement. Then we started finding more pieces of this animal. There were giant pieces of tentacles with suction cups all around us as we sailed along.

What we had experienced was listening to the life-and-death battle between a sperm whale and a giant squid. There could have been more than one whale. Something we took for granted was pretty eerie when we actually witnessed it.

In *Warriors of the Rainbow*, one of the Greenpeace books, there was a mention of finding giant squid pieces out in the ocean. They took it on board, put it in the freezer and had all the seafood they could eat. They didn't say how it tasted.

We were just in the right place at the right time to sail through the arena where that battle took place.

A Jules Verne story came true in our lives. ✍

Whales Come
To Boats

Curiosity

*In 1975, **Eddie DeJesus** and his wife decided that they were going to change their lifestyles. They could see themselves being caught up in the materialistic society around them. They were spending more time working to support the things that they had. Eddie says they saw the trap of that system: if they continued, they would have even more and enjoy it even less.*

So, they sold their house, both cars and almost everything they owned. They bought a sailboat and went cruising, and have never been the same. Eddie says that it may sound trite, but it seems to him to be a more natural existence; treading more lightly on this Earth. For example, they know they can survive on 75 gallons of water a month; most Americans use that much in half a day and are unaware of it.

We all make our choices and decisions about the way we want to live. Eddie and his wife are really happy with what they are doing. They both have marketable skills, so they work a little and play a lot, which they say is a good balance for them.

My encounter was absolutely one of those moving experiences in life which many people feel by having close interactions with whales.

I was crewing on a Cutty Hunk 41 on its way from England to the United States in the winter of 1976-77, on the passage from the Canary Islands to Antigua. There were four of us aboard: the owner and his wife, another crew person and myself. We left Grand Canary just before Christmas for a voyage that was to take 28 days. We averaged about a hundred miles a day and were about halfway across.

Just after sunrise, with good light in the sky, I was on watch and saw a whale's blow. Two whales were off our starboard quarter, a third to a half a mile away. I don't know what kind of whales they were. Shortly after the trip I looked at a lot of whale images, but I never came to a firm conclusion about what they were.

We were heading almost due west and they were headed north, traveling about 90 degrees away from us. I stood up in the cockpit to see them better. I was stunned by what they did.

They turned.

In my mind they absolutely and unquestionably deliberately stopped and turned toward the boat. Rather than making me feel afraid or causing any fear, it was apparent to me that these whales were curious about us.

Both of them swam over to the boat. They came alongside and swam parallel to our course, about 15 to 20 feet away. They were each a little less than the length of the boat, perhaps 35 or 36 feet long.

What was really awe-inspiring was that they would get right up alongside the boat, one at a time. One would roll on its side, flipper in the air, and you could see this big eye just looking the boat over. You could watch the eye move along the boat, from stern to bow and back.

The first whale would roll up and look, then roll down underwater, swim in a circle and get behind the second whale who did the same thing. Each whale made three passes of the boat, looking us over. Maybe they wondered who made our sails or some other detail about the boat.

We were all on deck. Watching them, we never felt any sense of danger. The boat was under sail; we never started the engine or made noises. Each one of them made their three leisurely passes inspecting us. Then the whales broke off and continued swimming to wherever they were going.

I've always, always remembered this: it was very moving. There was no doubt in my mind that those animals were curious. They stopped where they were going, they came over, looked at us and left. I could feel their intelligence at that moment.

I can't say there was communication, but these were intelligent creatures. There was never a question that they might bump the boat; nothing like that occurred to us. They just wanted to see what we were.

It was almost 20 years ago.

I still remember it clearly. ◁

Don't Eat That!

Bill Howell and his wife Laura left on a sailing circumnavigation of the world two weeks after they were married in 1979. It was their first ocean sailing experience together. Bill had done some blue water sailing, but Laura had never been on a sailboat before they met, a year earlier.

They spent about 18 months going across the South Pacific, then lived in Australia for three years. It took them another year to cross the Indian Ocean. They next spent five years in Africa. They left there and sailed north to the Caribbean where their first child was born. Then they returned to the United States.

Theirs was a leisurely trip, as they kept running out of money and needed to work in between passages. Bill worked in the computer industry as an information technology consultant, while Laura managed a yacht chandlery and went to school. They now have a 36-foot boat, which they built in Australia. They also have two children and hope to return to the world cruising community when the kids are a little older.

In 1980 we were making a passage between Bora Bora and Tonga in a 28-foot sloop. Ours was a small, simple boat: no engine and virtually no electronics.

In order to assist us in our celestial navigation and dead reckoning we towed a Walker Log. This is a mechanical device which tells us the distance the boat has traveled. It consists of a metered dial mounted on the stern, and a rotator which is towed some distance behind the boat. The rotator spins, causing the meter to turn.

Sometimes the rotator is eaten by large fish, so we carried several spares just in case.

We maintained a continuous watch, so there was always someone on deck. One afternoon we saw a pod of whales a hundred yards away from us, traveling in the same direction we were. We assumed they were pilot whales, as they had very round heads, with the largest whale something over 25 feet. Big, but not huge.

That largest one, which I presumed was a male, peeled off from the pod and swam over more directly towards where we were sailing. It was as if he came over to check out who we were. Or, to make sure that we were not a danger, or food, or whatever.

As he swam towards us, Laura and I both looked back and said, "Oh, gosh, we've got this Walker Log spinning out there. Is the whale going to think this is like a fishing lure? Is he going to take a bite of that?"

He didn't. He angled away from us and swam back to where the rest of his pod was.

By now the pod was catching up to us and getting very close, probably 25 to 30 feet off our starboard side. We could see that there was the one big male, at least one female, and a couple of what looked like teenagers. There was also a baby.

All of a sudden, the baby left the pod, came over to the Walker Log, and put his mouth around it. Literally, he put his lips around the spinning rotator. Neither of us knew what was going to happen. Just as the baby closed his mouth around the Walker Log, the big male swam over and gently but soundly rammed his head into the baby's tummy.

It was like when a human baby spits her nuggie or binkie, the thing they suck, out of their mouth. The baby whale sort of went "Phuh!" and out came the rotator. The little baby then swam quickly back to its mother and began to nurse.

The human analogy was really like the family walking down the sidewalk, and the little 12-month old who has just learned how to walk goes over and picks up the cigarette butt or chewing gum off the sidewalk, and puts it in his mouth. The daddy whacks his backside, and the kid spits it out and runs back to mommy for comfort.

All of this took place very quickly, but it was just exactly like an encounter with a human family going by on a Sunday afternoon walk around the park.

As it turned out, the baby whale did not abrade the line that holds the rotator or bend any of the fins which make it spin. It was a pretty incredible experience for us.

We saw other whales on our voyage around the world, but none so closely as these. ✍

I Wonder Why?

Rick Wolworth sails as much as he can. This year he got a boat of his own to sail in the Caribbean; he may be there right now.

I've told this story often when conversations turn to what we have seen at sea.

Over the last couple of years, I've been delivering boats from Trinidad up into the States. On one trip, we were two days out of St. Thomas, in the ocean on a 36' Pearson cutter. There were three of us on board.

The other two guys were below: the owner, a young guy; and Spike, whom we picked up in St. John. I was on deck alone.

I was in the cockpit and saw something strange in the water, and screamed what I believe people have yelled out from the beginning of time: "There's a whale!"

The whale came over to the boat. It was cool. Man, he was big! What I could see of him, he was probably about two thirds as long as the boat, maybe 25 feet long. The tail part of him was under the water. Not being familiar with whales, I don't know what kind of whale it was.

He swam over, perpendicular to the boat, with his head right by the cockpit. We made eye contact. Shortly after making eye contact with me, the whale did a complete 360-degree roll in the water, spinning with his body still perpendicular to the boat. His head remained by the cockpit, and he made this 360, keeping his head towards the boat. When he came up we made eye contact again, and he then rolled another 360 degrees, parallel to the boat.

He spun right by the boat. And when he was completely upside down, he took a dump.

It looked like a big mess in the water. And for all I know about whales, they could always do it upside down, though I did think it was kind of a unique experience. Now, I ask you; do you suppose that whale took one look at me, and...? I just don't know.

At that point, the owner came out and was concerned. Having heard stories about whales, and the possibility of a whale having a problem, and being insecure about being offshore for the first time, he started the engine, although he didn't put it in gear.

Apparently reacting to the sound of the engine or the owner's vibrations, the whale left. Slowly he continued his path.

The whale definitely made eye contact with me. He was close; we were within feet of each other. Then he was spinning around, before he took a big dump. I'm still not sure just exactly what that means.

The whale had a fairly narrow head. It seems to me like there was a hump, or something, in his back. But I have to admit that I was kind of overwhelmed by the whole presence of that animal.

I had always wanted to see a whale. For years, I'd be out in the Bay of Fundy or wherever and go to these different stations where people were watching whales. They would always say I just missed them, and I never saw one. It was quite an experience for me to see a whale at last, even though he did what he did.

I never figured out what kind of whale this one was, but the experience was more important to me than what species it really was that I saw.

It was a blast. ⌣

Greetings In The Galapagos

Richard A. Stanford *is a zoologist who visited the Galapagos Islands with his wife Edith to view the flora and fauna.*

On January 11, 1979, while sailing from Isabella to Duncan Islands in the Galapagos Islands, David Day, the naturalist on board, spotted a whale. He shouted the sighting to us while we were below having lunch. Everyone scrambled on deck, and sure enough, a whale was approaching the schooner! It was a Bryde's whale, between 40 and 50 feet long.

We saw the whale swim by the boat. When he was broadside to us, he rolled over on his back and swam belly-up. He gained speed and went ahead of the boat, then submerged out of sight for a few seconds.

David, who had climbed to the top of the mast to get a better view, would shout the position of the whale each time he came to the surface. We saw the whale again approaching from the stern. As the whale swam towards us, he would occasionally blow and come in quite close to the dinghy trailing behind the boat. Several times the whale went through the maneuver of approaching from astern, swimming on one side and passing far ahead. Each time the whale passed, he got closer to the boat. After tiring of this, he focused his attention on the dinghy.

The whale approached the dinghy and nudged it with his head. Needless to say, the excitement on board was growing to a frenzy, so much so that Gundi Day, the naturalist's daughter, decided to get into the dinghy. Bernhard Schreyer, the captain, pulled the small boat in close to the stern and Gundi hopped onboard.

The whale again approached from the stern, swimming very close to the dinghy. Gundi reached over as if to touch the whale, and the animal responded by moving closer to her.

Then it happened!

The whale moved in under Gundi's hand and she reached down to touch him. Everyone on the sailboat was amazed. The antic was repeated several times. Although we thought this was an incredible thrill, we were totally unprepared for what followed.

The whale was abeam of the boat; he approached the stern of the boat, where everyone was gleefully assembled. He came right alongside the boat, within five feet of the hull. The whale then swam past the boat, eyeing each one of us as he went by. The whale came so close to the stern that it seemed he wished everyone could touch his body; Gundi, in the dinghy, is the only one who did.

The encounter appeared to us as if the whale knew exactly what he was doing: seeking out human contact. The close interaction lasted approximately one hour and fifteen minutes.

Captain Schreyer said that in his thirty years of sailing the waters of the Galapagos Islands, he had never witnessed anything like this whale encounter before. ◁

Swimming
With Whales

At Last!!!

Michelle and Kevin Marsden live in the Gulf Islands of British Columbia. They have been actively sailing since 1979. In 1985 they launched "Teddy," a 42-foot, steel, gaff-rigged schooner they built. "Teddy" has carried them most recently to Central America, Hawaii, and back to B.C. They have temporarily "swallowed the anchor," and are living in a house they built which looks like a boat. Michelle manages the local dock for the Fisheries and Oceans Department, and also voluntarily leads a marine conservation project which includes a seal pup rescue program and an annual beach cleanup. Kevin builds houses and works on "Teddy." They have two sons and go sailing, and, of course, whale watching, as often as possible.

Our friend John was always and forever trying to see whales, but he never did. He would always miss them.

Many times the local orcas would go by just before John arrived, or just after he left. His timing was consistently off: he went out on whale watching charters in Tofino, B.C., and other places, but never saw one whale; he always got skunked. This went on for a couple of years.

He spent a lot of time on and around the water, working as a radio man for the Rescue Coordination Center in Victoria and with the Armed Forces in Comox, B.C., but still never saw a whale. He could laugh about his bum luck in failing to see a whale, but it was really frustrating for him.

Finally, John sailed south, as did my husband, Kevin, and I. We were anchored with a dozen other boats in a bay near Cabo San Lucas in Baja, Mexico. John decided to go scuba diving and look for the grate to the barbecue which he had lost overboard. So he put on his gear, and over he went.

Just after John went underwater, we saw a small humpback whale come into the outer anchorage. Not a baby: maybe it was a young female.

It was so typical. John had missed seeing yet another whale.

The whale came into the inner harbor where we were anchored and swam by all the boats. She came right by the stern of our boat, then swam by the stern of John's boat. She was diving down and coming up to the surface. And we thought, "John's probably seeing this down there. He's finally seeing his whale!"

Then we wondered where John was. We looked around and saw his air bubbles moving across the bay, following the same

route as the whale's surfacings. John stayed down 45 minutes, right to the very end of his air.

John surfaced at last by our boat. He was in total ecstasy. "You won't believe it! You won't believe it! I rubbed shoulders with a humpback whale!" he shouted. Years of disappointment had been vanquished. He had seen, swum with, and had been touched by a whale, at last!

He told us what happened:

John had been pawing through the sand under his boat for the lost barbecue grate, when he sensed something near him.

He looked up and was eyeball to eyeball with the whale!

She was within ten feet of him, watching him through the crystal clear water. John forgot all about the grate and began to swim with the young whale. They swam all around the bay together for 45 minutes.

At one point, the whale swam so close to John that she rubbed against his shoulder.

When he got back to the boat he was just ecstatic. He was in heaven, and he could not express himself coherently for hours. We were all truly happy for him.

It was our sense that the whale was in the harbor out of curiosity. She wasn't lost or feeding, just checking out the boats, and fulfilling John's wildest dreams about seeing a whale. She came in, threaded her way through the ten or twelve boats anchored in the bay, swam with John, and left when he got out of the water.

John sailed on to New Zealand in his boat "Baron Rouge."

He never did find the barbecue grate.

Oops!!!

Tom Callinan has been involved with the Cetacean Society International since the early 1970s.

Tom is a professional folksinger, songwriter and story teller. Proclaimed as the first Official State Troubadour of Connecticut, he is a member of The Morgans, a singing group specializing in songs of the sea. Tom travels with his musical messages about environ-

mental education, using history, humor, and harmony to share his thoughts and feelings about whales and our planet.

We often go out on whale watches.

The boat we usually are on is about 100 feet long. One time, a good friend of mine decided he would get into the water wearing a wetsuit to see if he could swim with the whales. Everyone, including a marine biologist, wanted to see what would happen, and to get some pictures. Our intention was not to harass the whales, but to see how they would react to a human swimming near them.

We found several humpbacks and slowly cruised among them for a while. My friend decided it was time for his experiment, so he jumped off the boat.

He no sooner got into the water than all the whales that had been around us swam away!

We told him he couldn't get back in the boat because he had chased away the whales that we had come to see. We said it was really remarkable to us to see what good taste those whales had! We kidded him mercilessly for the rest of that weekend, and longer. Every time I think of it, it is very, very funny.

He immediately got out of the water and was very embarrassed and apologetic.

We went in the whales' direction and approached them slowly, and did get to see them again, but we never got back among them in quite the same way. We told him it was all his fault.

It was even funnier when I called him recently to ask his approval for releasing this information about him.

He declined to be named; though he did tell me that when he got into the water, the humpbacks all lifted up their flukes, then pooped on him. He said he was swimming through a brown cloud as the whales turned and swam away from him. He had a wetsuit on, so none of their droppings got on his skin.

As I said, he will remain nameless. ✍

Don't Go!

Anne Collet, a French marine scientist, also tells the story on page 98, in which she was in the water with a dying whale.

I was in Argentina studying right whales, which are sometimes very playful with people.

A right whale came up to me while I was diving, skin diving with no air tanks. This was the first time I had ever been swimming with a right whale, and it was quite impressive. I stayed with the whale for about half an hour, then decided to go back to my rubber boat.

The whale came up to me, looked at me, and passed just under my feet. I was afraid I might hurt her with my large swim fins.

As I was climbing into the boat, the whale just turned over and looked at me again, and I'm sure she knew exactly what she was doing. She turned on her side so the flukes of her tail were vertical; she rose up underneath me and carried me away from the boat! I was riding on a whale!

She had taken me off our rubber boat. I didn't know what to do!

Then the whale dove deeper, and I floated to the surface. It had only been 20 seconds or so, but the whale ride seemed like a very long time.

After I got into the boat and was leaving the area, the whale followed us as if we were in a parade. It seemed like she did not want us to go away. The whale then began to breach, leaping completely out of the water. During fifteen minutes she breached twelve times, landing with a big splash.

It is a beautiful memory I have from diving with these whales, a surprising interaction with a big animal. ⊲

Contact Made!

Ross Isaacs *has over twenty years of experience as a diver work-ing around the world in a wide variety of situations. A freelance underwater cinematographer and marine naturalist, Ross has worked extensively with marine mammals during the past de-cade. He has produced a number of documentary films and books; his latest book is "Encounters With Whales."*

Ross hopes that by helping to fuel the groundswell of com-passion towards whales and the ocean environment through his projects, we can reverse historic human behavior so as to ensure our survival on Earth.

The following is an excerpt from "Encounters With Whales."

The sun hit the broken surface and smashed into a million beams moving continuously in a dancing veil of monochromatic blue rhythms. I drifted along, straining my ears to hear the singer, and focused my eyes into the blue haze, hoping the behemoth would approach me. I started my "whale call," emitting strange and amusing sounds through the end of my snorkel. I felt some-what foolish, but knew this was my best chance to attract an in-quisitive whale at close range. As I stared into the empty depths, the sunbeams seemed to converge into one point some distance away at the edge of my visibility. Small semi-transparent inverte-brates undulated amongst the shafts of light occasionally piercing their living protoplasm in an ethereal dance of cosmic forms.

Suddenly, a large shape materialized at the vortex of the sun-beams. Eye to eye, gliding weightless towards this colossal mam-mal, I watched pensively as the forty-ton humpback whale ap-proached. The eye widened as the leviathan gently rolled over on her back, like some great playful dinosaur, maneuvering her im-mense mass in closer to ponder my insignificant presence.

Overawed at first, I cowered, hiding behind my Zodiac, which would afford little protection against this monumental animal should she become agitated.

Inquisitively, she followed me to my side of the boat, which bobbed like a rubber duck in a bathtub. I stopped filming and for a fleeting moment I reached out my open hand to the great crea-ture in a gesture of trust. To my complete amazement, she swung her two-ton, fifteen foot long pectoral fin around, placing it into my hand!

I shivered with excitement as her large bulging eye connected with mine in some strange recognition of consciousness. At that moment I came to the realization that I was swimming with an animal possessing a brain, driven by more than just the basic instinct to eat, reproduce and survive.

She swung her enormous head towards me, her chin only centimeters from my camera. I was tempted to reach out and pick a tiny whale louse from her lip as some kind of memento. Instead, I continued filming, capturing some of the closest footage ever recorded, revealing their inquisitive nature.

Knowing our species has almost decimated their numbers, I am humbled as these animals transcend our trivial human needs and impulses of greed. The humpback whale is a majestic creature, a true giant of its blue domain. Almost grotesque in appearance because of its huge bulk and numerous protrusions, it is also strangely appealing, so much so that its plight has become a cause close to the hearts of all human beings and perhaps the greatest symbol of conservation of our time.

This was to be my most extraordinary encounter with a whale. The animal actually stayed with our Zodiac long enough for me to board the inflatable, dry the underwater camera housing, and reload my movie camera three times. The images from this encounter are some of the most unique and significant to date. ⚓

© Ross Isaacs/Ocean Planet Images®

They Want To See Us Too

Susan Dummit and her pathologist husband Steve live in North Carolina. They have a 30-foot "Seasprite" which they sail in Pamlico Sound. They sail often in the Caribbean and occasionally go to other parts of the world with their sailing friends, chartering bareboats.

In 1991, we were bareboat sailing in Tonga.

We had seen spouts and breaching in the distance, so we knew whales were in the area. We had been told at Moorings, the yacht charter company, that if we wanted to get in the water with the whales, it would be fine, not to worry about it. We were pretty sure they were humpback whales on their migration from Alaska.

Sailing into a huge bay, with miles of water around us, we saw spouts ahead of us. We turned the motor on and got over to the whales as quickly as we could. They seemed to be leading us on, into the bay.

Finally, they seemed interested in us, and swam around near our boat. There were five of them; perhaps a mama, a daddy, a baby, and two adolescents, judging from their sizes. The baby was suckling.

There were seven of us on the boat: my husband Steve, sons Clarke and Steve, Jr., nephew Preston, and friends Liz and Bill Gibson. Liz and I stayed on the boat to take care of it while the guys all dinghied out to where the whales were. One guy would stay in the dinghy and the other four would swim with the whales. They swam with them for about an hour.

My son was swimming with the mama and the baby, real close to them. He really wanted to touch the baby and was about to, when he remembered that they were mammals. He did not want to threaten them, so he stroked the mother instead.

The whales seemed to be as interested to be with us as we were to be with them.

After swimming with the men, the whales became interested in our 50-foot sailboat. The whales had been off at a distance from the boat, but now they came over and swam in front of us, then swam under the bow to come up on the other side. We were probably going three or four knots at that time.

The whales seemed to be playing with us in an investigative sort of way. The baby made us hysterical. He would dive under the bow and come up like he was standing on his tail, spyhopping. He appeared absolutely gleeful to us.

When my husband was in the dinghy coming back to the sailboat, he was on a converging course with the largest whale. From the deckhouse, I had a really good view into the water, but my husband in the dinghy did not. I could see that he and the whale were on a collision course and I didn't know what was going to happen.

Apparently the whale knew where the dinghy was the whole time. In order to avoid running into it, he breached right in front of it. He bent almost in two to keep his tail from coming down onto the dinghy. I was terrified for a minute, then it was obvious that the whale knew where the dinghy was and what he had to do to avoid it.

The whales swam around the boat for about twenty minutes. They did a lot of breaching, really close to us.

It was a fascinating experience. Liz and I never got into the water with the whales, but we could see really well from the boat. It was fun to watch the interaction between the whales and the guys in the water. When the whales came really close to the sailboat and dove under the bow, I was running up and down all over the boat.

We were the only boat in this very large bay, in the Vava U Islands in northern Tonga. ◁

Feeding
The Animals

Feeding Orcas Off Africa

Marcelino Alberola Alves' family had a small fleet of fishing boats based in Casablanca, Morocco: three trawlers 100 feet long and two smaller sardine seine boats. He was the chief engineer/mechanic for the fleet and worked on all the boats, rotating among them doing maintenance while they were out at sea fishing.

In the years 1973-75 our boats were fishing in the waters between the Canary Islands, Morocco and Muritania. We were trawling, dragging huge nets along the ocean floor at 120-200 fathoms. The bottom was flat, but sloping and muddy. Our goal was to catch sole, turbot and shrimp. We also caught young white octopus; in fact, we caught more octopus than fish. After a five-hour trawl, when we hauled in the net it held eight tons. Five of those tons were the young octopus, four to six inches long.

The 16 crew members would gather and shovel these octopus back into the ocean. They were waste to us, for at the time there was no market for them. It is all different now, but then we threw them all back into the ocean.

And orca whales would come to eat the octopus.

We would be out fishing for three to seven days, depending on the catch. The orcas would find us and circle around us, three to four whales, swimming in large circles while we towed the net. After the catch was hauled in and we began to shovel the octopus overboard, those orcas would come alongside the boat, sometimes touching it.

When we tossed the shovel full of octopus into the air, they would squirt out black "ink" which fell onto the boat and into the water. The orcas would catch them with their mouths wide open before the octopus hit the water. Sometimes we would just empty a shovel full of octopus right into a whale's mouth when they were close to the boat. When the orcas had their fill, they would swim away, but they would be back for more as long as we were out fishing.

We saw them on every trip in April and sometimes in September of those three years. They would find us while we were towing the trawl and wait to be fed. I always felt that it was a pity not to have taken any photographs of it, but we were there to fish, not to take snapshots.

As I said, today it is all different. All the boats have freezer tanks. There are 200-mile coastal fishing limits. And, there is a big market in Asia for young octopus now. Both Japan and Korea have

boats fishing in these waters catching the young octopus to freeze and take home.

I don't know what these orcas eat. Maybe those octopus were just a special treat for them. That is the only "throwback" fish that ever brought the whales to us.

It was an amazing experience to be feeding those fierce-looking, wild animals just like puppy dogs.

I'll never forget it. ✍

Feeding Orcas In Washington

V. A. Luckhurst is from Dillingham, Alaska, and has fished quite a bit in Alaska, especially at Bristol Bay and Cook Inlet. Now he just hangs gear, getting other fishermen's nets ready. He also is a carpenter. V. A. enjoys going back to Alaska in the spring to hang gear, because it is fun work and he gets to visit with his old friends and family there again. He also shares the tale on page 44.

One summer, Bill Catlow and I were out trolling for salmon off Lime Kiln Point on San Juan Island.

We saw all these killer whales coming, maybe fifty of them. We were right in their path.

I talked Bill into shutting the motor off. The whales kept getting closer and closer. Bill started to panic. He thought they were going to come and get us, maybe even get in the boat, because they were jumping out of the water and slamming down pretty good. They were just coming up all over.

I laughed at his fears, and calmed him down because I knew that these whales left people alone.

I told him, "They aren't going to bother us. Just tap on the boat and let them know we're here." I started tapping on the boat and talking to the whales. The orcas came all around the boat. They were rolling, and going up on their tails (spyhopping).

Then this skiff, an old planked skiff with a nine-horse Johnson outboard motor on it, came out. There was an older fellow and a young girl in it. They came out and the whales went right over to them. He shut his little motor off, and the whales would come up to the stern of the boat.

The girl would dump herring in their mouths. They were feeding them! A whale came right up to the boat and the people gave them some fish. It would eat, and then another whale would come up to get fed. The people would give them each a little taste. The whales were just all around them. It was amazing.

Those folks must have done that before because the whales went right over to them, like they recognized the boat and the people. The whales surrounded our boat again, coming up on their tails...when another boat came out fast and scared them all off. ✍

Collisions

Quick Stop!

Terry Nicolls works at Newport News Shipbuilding in Virginia, where he's a radiological control supervisor, responsible for radiation safety. With 22,000 employees, Newport News Shipbuilding is the largest private shipyard in America. They can build any type of ship, including nuclear submarines. They are the only shipyard in the U.S. that can build nuclear aircraft carriers.

Terry has owned nine sailboats, from a Sunfish to a custom Ron Holland 40. He sold "No Justice," the boat in the following story, to a Canadian sailor. His present boat is a Carrera 290.

We were doing a race in Hampton Roads Harbor, a sailboat race in the Hampton Yacht Club's Frost Bite Series. I had a friend of mine, Rob Pierce, at the tiller of my 38-foot custom Farr, and I was trimming the spinnaker.

We could see a lot of police cars and fire trucks up on the beach. We couldn't really be sure what was going on, but it was unusual. We were not paying too much attention to them because we were racing, and we could not imagine that what they were doing related to us in any way.

I was trimming the spinnaker and we were sailing along fast when a Coast Guard cutter comes up to us. He was saying something over the loudspeaker, but we couldn't understand the words, so we sailed out of their way.

What had happened was that the fire department and the Coast Guard had gotten a sick whale off the beach, a whale that had washed up. The Coast Guard cutter was trying to herd that whale out of the bay, and was warning us about it.

So, standing up on deck trimming the sail, I had a lot better view than everybody else. I saw a fin coming through the water, like a dolphin's fin or something. Nobody else saw it but me.

All of a sudden the fin disappeared.

Even more suddenly, we stopped.

It was like a car crash. I fell down and everybody else was thrown forward. We went from over six knots to zero instantly. It was like a big crash in a movie, lots of noises: the rigging clanging, sails flapping, people rolling around in the cockpit all over each other wondering what the heck happened.

When I saw the fin, I was looking on the port side. After I fell down, I was looking on the starboard side, and saw this broad expanse of back. "Damn! We hit a whale! That's all it could be! We hit a whale!"

My crew did not believe me, and no one ashore believed us either. "There are no whales here," they said.

But that was what happened. And no one believed us. "Yeah, right. You hit a whale. You must have had a lot to drink today." We didn't do very well in that race, which was unusual since my boat, "No Justice," was high point champion that season.

The next day the newspaper had an article about this sick whale that had washed up. They wrote about our boat failing to heed the Coast Guard's warning, and how we hit the whale. People are real sensitive about whales here. We did not know what the Coast Guard was doing; it was just a big misunderstanding. We did not *want* to hit that whale.

On the following day the newspaper had another article all about the whale. It was a fin whale: at 60,000 pounds, one of the biggest whales in the ocean. The whale was in Hampton Roads Harbor because it was sick. As the whale repeatedly came into the harbor, the Coast Guard kept trying to herd it out into the ocean again.

This went on for several days. The whale kept beaching itself and eventually they put it to sleep. The local marine biologists and veterinarians did an autopsy on it and said that the whale had chronic kidney disease. The second newspaper article said that we did not hurt the whale by hitting it with the sailboat.

We may not have hurt the whale, but we did hurt my boat: about $2,000 worth of damage, including separating the keel-to-hull joint.

I was a little upset, because the way they wrote the first article in the paper made it sound like the reason the whale was sick was because my boat hit him, and that wasn't the case at all. The second article they wrote was more accurate.

Every once in a while someone will still ask, "Say, aren't you the guy that hit the whale?"

And that was in 1987. ✒

Take That!

Don Anderson *is a senior research scientist for Chevron Oil, where he has worked since 1960, when he earned his PhD in chemistry at the University of Illinois. A citizen of the United Kingdom, Don has plans to enjoy world cruising with his wife in their Valiant 47 when he retires in a few years.*

On Saturday, April 27, 1985, fellow Balboa Yacht Club member Rennie Storey and I, along with local sailors Bob Howie, Dave Kirchner, and Bill McNaughton, were crew for Jack Mallinckrodt aboard his Newport 41 sloop "Swift" in the annual Newport, California, to Ensenada, Mexico, race.

We were the second class to start and got away with clean air at the leeward end of the line. The wind was light from the south and remained that way until sunset when we were about ten miles off Oceanside. During the night we had occasional wind shifts to the west and north which allowed us to get the spinnaker up a few times.

By dawn Sunday we were south of the border a few miles off Tijuana. We could see about ten other contestants scattered about the ocean within five miles of us. We were beating south in a gentle southeasterly breeze about a mile off Rosarito Beach. Seas were smooth and we were making about five knots.

Suddenly there was a loud "Thump!" and the boat stopped dead in the water. My first thought was that we had hit a submerged log; we were too far offshore to have run aground. I was about to check the bilge below the cabin sole for any sign of leaks when there came an even more horrendous "THUMP!"

This time the whole boat shuddered and the mast and rigging vibrated violently as though it were about to go over the side.

At the same time, the stern of the boat was lifted about six feet out of the water.

The wheel was wrenched from the helmsman and spun freely. We were dead in the water without steerage way and without any rudder control.

We realized that we had run into a California gray whale which had been resting just beneath the surface, and he had then attacked the stern of our boat. No sooner had we determined the cause of the upset than the whale attacked twice more in rapid succession from astern, each time ramming us with his head.

The giant animal then came at us a fourth time, again from astern, but this time he dove beneath the boat, raising his eight foot wide tail high above us. This action dumped gallons of water into the cockpit and down the companionway into the cabin. We were all soaked. The tail struck the transom of the boat, knocking one of the ventilator cowls off its mounting and dislodging the man-overboard pole from its deck socket.

The whale then sounded, leaving us with the eerie silence of a sailing vessel motionless on a smooth sea. All that remained of his presence was a large smooth swirl on the ocean's surface astern of us. The entire encounter lasted less than one minute.

Nothing had been said or done by the crew except for, "Oh, my God!" uttered by skipper Mallinckrodt when he realized we were about to be attacked by a whale larger than the boat. We were all utterly surprised and dumbfounded. The helmsman just stood in disbelief with his hands outstretched, about a foot away from the wheel which had been torn from his hands moments earlier.

We now set about assessing the damage. The first thing was to determine whether the hull had been holed; a serious leak would have meant abandoning the vessel and taking to the inflatable liferaft. All seemed sound, so we dropped the jib and began repairing the steering gear.

Jack and I crawled under the cockpit and found the rudder quadrant swinging freely. The whale had buckled a six-inch diameter bronze pulley and stripped the heavy stainless steel cable from the steering gear. We were able to straighten the pulley, remove most of the kinks in the cable, and put everything back together in about an hour. The jib was hoisted and we were soon underway again for Ensenada. The steering was a lot stiffer than usual since it seemed the whale had bent the rudder shaft.

We all felt very lucky that the encounter with the whale had been in daylight and under very mild weather conditions. Also, we were most fortunate that the whale had attacked from the stern rather than from the side of the boat; a ram from the side would surely have holed the boat, and it would probably have sunk in less than a minute.

As we approached Ensenada we debated amongst ourselves whether we should tell anyone about our encounter with the gray whale. Would anyone believe us?

But the story reached the town before we did. Another yacht had been about 500 yards from us and witnessed the event. The skipper of this San Diego yacht carried the news to Ensenada, reporting that the whale was larger than our 41-foot sailboat. The skipper had called us several times on the radio to see if we needed assistance, but we were too busy looking for tools and making repairs to listen to the radio.

We crossed the finish line at the Ensenada harbor breakwater on Sunday afternoon, then headed back immediately for Newport Beach. We had a good westerly breeze and so made good time up the coast, arriving in Newport at 2 a.m. on Tuesday. We saw no more whales.

Collisions between sailboats and whales are not uncommon. Most often it's a glancing blow, and damage usually is not sustained. Power boats rarely collide with whales, presumably because engine and propeller noise warn the whale.

Attacks on vessels by whales are extremely rare, although they will sometimes come close to a boat in the ocean, apparently out of curiosity or interest. ⩗

Research

Whale Tales

A Good Job Well Done

Michael Williamson *teaches oceanography, marine biology and environmental science at Wheelock College in Massachusetts to future teachers. He is trying to have an exponential effect on environmental awareness with a program he has begun called "WhaleNet," an interdisciplinary teaching program on the Internet. Through it, teachers throughout the world can access research data and research groups, then use that information in their classrooms to enhance science and environmental awareness and education.*

Michael also serves as the Associate Director of the Mingan Island Cetacean Study (MICS), which has been working in the Gulf of Saint Lawrence for, he says, "quite a while." He shares this collection of remembrances:

We have been researching blue whales for about 17 years now. One of my most memorable times was when we were out in a 15-foot inflatable trying to photo-ID two blue whales and they both sounded, going opposite directions.

I was ready to photograph one of the whales when it next surfaced. What we didn't know was that there were *three* whales. I was looking through the viewfinder, focusing on this one animal, when I heard an explosion in my left ear.

I glanced over and this body was going by me as big as a wall. It was the third blue whale! I saw this huge eyeball go past, so close I could have put my hand on it.

My partner, Rich Sears, who is the Executive Director of MICS, gunned the motor and the boat zipped away. I lost my balance and took one step back to catch myself, and fell down. I knew if I took another step I would go over the stern.

After he picked me back up, I asked Rich why he gunned it. I could have taken this great picture of the whale's eye! He said, "Well, the whale went by on the left and its flipper went by on the right side of the boat. The flukes were coming, and they were about 25 feet across. If we didn't move we would have been aced by them."

Oh.

Just being that close to these animals was amazing.

With all the different species we see, we have many experiences. For instance, we were trying to photograph one particular minke whale. On this day I was driving and Sears was using the camera. The whale had an unusual marking we were trying to get a picture of, a big dent on his rostrum.

This minke was being very elusive, diving whenever we approached. After about an hour of trying to photograph the whale, we were both totally frustrated, so I shut down the motor. I happened to glance over my left shoulder and saw, after all this time, the whale spyhopping about five feet off our stern. He was watching *us*, and we were looking in the other direction.

I whispered, "Sears! Sears!" Rich turned around, and this big whale head was right there next to the boat. The prankster whale then actually put his mouth down in the water and blew bubbles at us. He went, "Phulluhh!" and then swam away. It was like, "Gotcha! Ha! Ha! Ha!"

A little later we did get the photo we wanted.

Every year there is something very special. Once, we were out with about 500 white-sided dolphins. They were all over the place, jumping and doing all the things dolphins do. Two of us, in two different boats, were about a mile away from the third, larger boat.

The dolphins poked their heads up and had a glint in their eyes, sort of like a Golden Retriever that has a stick in its mouth. They started going faster and faster, and we increased our speed to keep up with them. They would actually leap out of the water, look at us to check that we were still there, then go back down again. They were going so fast that they would skip on the surface of the water.

We were so intent on watching the dolphins that we weren't, at the time, paying attention to what direction we were going. They were leading us back to the third boat, right at them!

The people on the larger boat said they never saw us coming. They just saw about a dozen dolphins scream past them, two inflatables going at top speed right with them, watching the animals and the animals watching us.

We got about 50 yards beyond the big boat and the dolphins just stopped, turned around and looked at us. Like, "Thanks, that was cool." Then they left. They must have a sense of humor and an amazing acuity of what they are doing.

There is a whole spectrum of things that we have had the opportunity to see. In '83 or '84 there was a humpback whale named Ibis entrapped in a gill net. The net was about a quarter to a half a mile long, with two anchors and all the line. I was driving the boat with Parron Ross and Carol Carlson; Stormy Mayo was with us in another boat. We finally succeeded in getting Ibis unanchored from the bottom, but not out of the net. Then Ibis disappeared. We feared that she had drowned, because she just vanished. We had three boats and an airplane looking all over for her and we couldn't find her. We saw a big lump on the bottom with the depth sounder, and figured she had probably finally succumbed and sunk. But, actually, what we had done had unanchored her and she drifted away, still in the net.

About a month later they found Ibis off Provincetown. As you might imagine, she was extremely tired after dragging this net around for six or eight weeks.

David Matilla, Stormy, and many others worked to cut her free from the net. They couldn't get the line out of her mouth because she wouldn't open it. After about a half an hour, David Matilla got so frustrated that he just hit her in the head. Ibis then opened her mouth and they got the line out. He's the only person I know that punched out a whale!

Ibis had been dragging this mass of gear for two months during the feeding period. We were concerned that she might not survive the migration south, because of the lack of body fat or blubber. Ironic as it seems, the next year, on the first whale watch I went out on, there was Ibis, looking good!

By the time we got back to shore that day, we were relatively inebriated; every boat was carrying a bottle of champagne with them to celebrate whoever found Ibis first. You become semi-attached to some of these different critters that you've spent time with.

I guess I would be one of the "Old Guard," or at least the echelon in the middle because I started whale watching back in

1974 in Massachusetts. The "Old Ones" would be Bill Cheville and Bill Watkins, who worked out of Woods Hole, and people like that. Then there are my peers, and now there is a third generation of people who knew what they wanted to do when they went to college, unlike those of us who sort of happened into this strange world.

I met Rich Sears in 1977 while working at Mt. Desert Rock Lighthouse with Steve Katona. We talked it over and decided that because there were so many boats whale watching in Massachusetts, rather than be one of many doing the same thing, that we would venture more off into the field.

Rich came across a blue whale population in the Gulf of Saint Lawrence, and, since no one had studied it, we decided we would go that direction. As it turned out, we developed the method used to photo-identify blue whales. Our paper was published by the International Whaling Commission. As far as I know, anyone who studies blue whales now uses the method we developed.

It's like a marine mammal aquarium up there. We have blue, humpbacks, fins, minkes, orcas, pilot whales and an occasional sperm whale; whiteside and white beaked dolphins, harbor and gray seals. It's a big area: we travel up to 25 miles offshore, covering 80 to 120 miles a day or so in the inflatables. We go out of Lonsue Point, about 500 miles east of Quebec City, on the north shore of the Gulf of Saint Lawrence. We see groups of 10-20 fin whales traveling together; it is a wonderfully rich feeding ground for all these animals. We've photo-identified more than 300 blue whales over the past 15 years.

Having the skills, or experience, to identify individuals, we took blue whale research from a fishery science to a mammalian study, and can now learn more about social interactions of these animals because we are able to recognize individuals. For example, every year when a whale we call Laser shows up, Spindle arrives within a day or two. They tend to travel together.

By photo-identifying individuals you can really get to know some of their personalities. Every year, the first blue whale we identified, Pita, would show up within one day of August 15th.

"Pita" initially stood for "Pain-In-The-Ass." Because she was so difficult to photograph, it took us two hours to get the first quality image of her for the photo-id. Then she turned into a pain in the opposite way, she would follow us around, like a hundred and fifty-ton Saint Bernard. We would photograph her and go four or five miles away, and she would pop up again. We would move and she'd pop up again. We would yell, "Get out of here, Pita!"

Even when we were stopped in the water, she would swim by, then make an abrupt turn, come over and go right by us again.

Actually "she" turned out to be a "he." Pita washed in dead on Anticosti Island about two years ago, with no apparent cause of death. He was huge, which was one reason we thought he was a female. He must have been pretty old. It gives us a lot of input into our research, because we are wondering if there is a sexual or social dominance. We can go back through all our data and see whether Pita was first or second or third in these groupings of whales, and see if there was any consistency there.

So, even the death of Pita may shed more light in the behavior of these animals.

There is no end to the stories of things we've seen with the whales. A male humpback named Helix used to go nuts every time he went near Chantey, a female. They had a three-year relationship, which is unheard of for humpback whales. Usually a meaningful relationship might last 30 seconds. These two were together for three years.

Every time he went around Chantey, Helix would start breaching. If a whale could strut, Helix would strut. He came up under one of the inflatables once, rolled over and bounced the boat on his belly three times. Then he swam off. I thought it was pretty funny because I was in the other boat, watching.

It looked to me as if he was just showing off, flexing his muscles.

These days, Helix and Chantey have been sighted in the Gulf of Maine and they are totally separated. So there is a big change in the social relationship between those two whales, after this extended three-year jaunt.

I guess I made one of the first humpback "matches" between the Gulf of Maine and the Gulf of Saint Lawrence populations, matching ID photographs. I happened to have photos of the same whale in both places and I called Steve Katona, who was coordinating the humpback whale catalogue then.

I was excited to have found this match, but as it turned out I called almost to the minute that he had finished writing a paper in which he said that humpback whales had discrete populations. He asked me not to call him again until after the conference where he was going to present his paper! He did include the information I shared with him.

Since then, we've recorded lots of matches between the Western Gulf of Saint Lawrence and Massachusetts Bay humpback whales.

All this has opened a lot of windows about these animals; yet once you think you understand something about whales, they prove you wrong. ⤙

Calling The Whales

Hawaiian Magic

Lyndia and Lance Storey-Leonard divide their time between Lopez Island, Washington, and Kauai, Hawaii.

Lyndia's background includes running a radio station, being a lobbyist, doing social work, writing, and starting political and social programs. It took her a while, she says, to recognize the spiritual nature of the world because she saw such separation all around her. Now she says she sees the interconnectedness of all life.

Lance's life is about modeling a new paradigm of learning through joy, living with abundance, loving every day, and sharing with others. Everything he does revolves around that, including the building of a 42-foot Alden schooner.

Lyndia and Lance have a network marketing business selling spirulina.

On many evenings, our neighbors come to our house on Kauai to sit on our rock wall and watch the sunset. Often we see humpback whales there.

One particular night, our friends Jody and Victor came over. Jody was lamenting that her good friend, Joy, who was visiting from England, had come to Hawaii specifically because Jody had told her so much about the whales. For some reason, during the whole two weeks that Joy had been there, she had not seen even one whale. Joy really wanted to see a whale: she had gone on whale watching cruises, to whale watching spots, everything; there were never any whales wherever she went.

This was the last day of Joy's visit, and she was sitting in Jody's house feeling really disappointed. I said, "Jody, call her up and tell her to come over." Jody said, "Oh, you know, she's just so disappointed. I don't think she will." About that time some whales appeared in our view. I said, "Tell Joy to come right now, and she'll be able to see them."

There Joy was, just down the street in this little condo feeling badly because she had not seen any whales, and we were sitting there watching several humpbacks go by the house. They were not really that close, but we could see them.

In the time it took to get Joy to join us, the whales started leaving. They were really far away, swimming around the point where we couldn't see them. We could see their spouts and once in a while you'd see a tail, but by the time she got there the whales were by the point, and almost gone.

Jody said to me, "Now she is really, really going to be disappointed." I said, "Jody, don't worry, we'll call the whales and they'll come back. Because they always come if you call them."

Jody wasn't real sure about that, but then Joy came over to where we were sitting and I suggested that we all focus our energy on calling the whales and ask them to come back. We closed our eyes for a couple of minutes and silently asked them to return.

Shortly after we opened our eyes, the whales turned and started to come towards us! They kept swimming closer, and closer, and closer, until they were almost in front of our house. We felt they would probably keep going.

Then I suggested that we ask the whales to stop right in front of our house and give us a big show. I was feeling more confident about "talking to the whales."

We closed our eyes and asked them to come and do their "whale show" for us.

By then, there were people lining the street, which was right along the beach. There's an informal community there. Not all of the people know each other but they come there because the sunsets are so spectacular; they will drop what they're doing and walk down to watch the sunset, or the whales. There were quite a few people along the road that night.

So, we thanked the whales for coming back and asked them to do a show for us. They came in so close, closer than we had ever seen them before or since. I don't know how many there were, maybe a dozen or more.

What I do remember was not how many there were, but the way that they came right to us. The first time they went by, they were fairly far out and swimming parallel to the beach. When we asked them to come back they were swimming parallel to the beach again but much closer. Right after we asked them to stop and please give us a show, they stopped, turned 90 degrees and swam in towards our house.

It wasn't just that they came in real close; they actually stopped right in front of the house, turned, and came straight in.

Since I snorkel out there often, I know how deep the water is, 40 to 45 feet deep.

That evening the whales performed the most spectacular "whale show" any of us had ever seen. They were breaching and tail lobbing everywhere; we could see their entire bodies, including the lines on their pectoral fins. It was quite a lengthy show, so Joy got to see "her" whales really well before she returned to England.

Everyone clapped and cheered for the whales when they breached. It was really fun. We were amazed and humbled to see the whales do exactly what I suggested and we had asked of them. The neighbors still talk about it.

We heard through other people that we are referred to as "those people who talk to the whales." ⌇

Dying Whales

How I Broke My Foot

Anne Collet *is a biologist working with whales and dolphins in France. This has been her work since 1980.*

She is the Director of the Oceanographic Museum and Research Center for Marine Mammals in La Rochelle. She also tells the tale on page 69.

This is a sad story, even though there is some humor at the end. You see, in January, 1994, I broke my leg because a whale stepped on me.

It was, unfortunately, a stranded whale; a rather large fin whale, fifty eight feet long. The animal washed ashore at night in a winter storm. The whale was still alive, but very thin and obviously dying: not a very pleasant situation.

My role, unhappily, was to administer a lethal injection and kill the whale. It was the only "humane" thing we could do for this poor animal which was slowly dying on the beach. In order to kill the whale, I had to put a large hypodermic needle directly into its heart. The syringe was also quite big and full of a very dangerous poison.

I waded into the water, carefully holding the syringe, and tried to get alongside the animal near the area where its heart was located. The water was cold, something like forty degrees Fahrenheit.

Before I could get near the heart, I was in over my head, with large waves from the storm crashing all around me. We decided to pull the whale higher up onto the beach, but there was no way to hold onto it because the whale's skin was pretty slippery. While I was trying to put a rope around the tale fluke of the whale, I lost my footing and fell down in the waves. My feet went under the fluke, which then came heavily down on my leg.

Because of the cold water, I did not realize that my leg had been broken. Also, even though it hurt, when there are four hundred people around asking you to do something important, you just forget about yourself.

We succeeded in pulling the whale partway out of the water with the rope. At last, very sadly, I administered the fatal injection.

Whale Tales

When I got back home at four o'clock this Sunday morning, I was tired and my leg began to be very painful. I decided to go to the hospital and asked a friend to take me there.

French people don't know that whales may be found off our coast. So, I can tell you that when you arrive at four in the morning at a hospital and tell the nurses that your leg hurts because a whale has stepped it, they cannot believe that you are not completely drunk. This is about the time the discotheques are closing and people are now partying in the street.

The nurses called the head doctor who had asked me to tell him the whole story. He thought the nurses' disbelief about how I was injured was very funny. ⋈

Conscious Choice

Mary Getten *has worked with marine mammals since 1987. A naturalist for five years on whale watching boats in the San Juan Islands in Washington and also in Maui, Hawaii, Mary serves as one of the coordinators of the Marine Mammal Stranding Network in San Juan County, Washington.*

She also has worked at The Whale Museum in Friday Harbor, Washington, in their research department. She has rewritten their book "Gentle Giants Of The Sea," an elementary school curriculum about whales.

This happened in the late '80s, probably about 1989, when I was working at the Marine Mammal Center in Sausalito, California.

The Center is mainly a hospital for seals and sea lions, but occasionally we dealt with stranded cetaceans. We had rescued two infant beaked whales that had stranded in San Francisco. They had been transported to Marine World Africa-USA, to the rehab tank there.

After about two weeks, one of the whales died. The other one was still alive a week later when I came on shift at one o'clock in the morning. (We gave the animals 24-hour care.)

This whale had been acting erratically all night, but was quite conscious and aware. There were three of us on duty. One person was in the pool just being there and watching what was happening. I was counting respirations, keeping track of the whale's breaths.

After a while the whale started swimming as fast as he could, doing laps around and around the pool. The woman in the pool got scared and said, "I'm getting out of here."

As she tried to get out, the whale crashed into her and hit the stairs.

This was something he had never done; he always seemed to be totally aware of where he was. The woman got out of the pool, and the whale just kept on doing laps, and doing laps, and doing laps, as fast as he could go. It was almost as though he was trying to swim right out of the pool.

I was still counting respirations, but he had completely stopped breathing. He kept swimming at full speed without breathing for fifteen minutes, just going as absolutely fast as he could go. He never took a breath.

Finally, the whale completely wore himself out, went into a barrel roll, and sank down to the bottom, dead.

It was amazing because it was really clear that this whale had consciously decided to die. He held his breath and swam full speed until his life's energy was gone.

One of the women that was there that night saw another whale do the same thing two months later. This time it was a pigmy sperm whale. She said he did the exact same thing. Both those whales made that choice. They held their breath and swam until their bodies gave out.

It was an amazing experience to be there and watch this intelligent animal's suicide, to see the awareness that he had and to witness what he was doing.

His was a conscious choice and a total "going for it."

Examining Astra

Lynn Hamilton *teaches literature and writing at the Savannah College of Art and Design. She lives on a small barrier island on the coast of Georgia, which she says is as close to paradise as she can imagine.*

I was at a Marine Center on Florida's west coast in December, 1994, participating in a dolphin study with Earthwatch.

The research has been going on for twenty years. They tag dolphins for study: the tags only stay on for ten minutes. Photographs are taken of the dolphins, which can be identified by the notches left by the tags.

My job was to drive around the bay with others in the study, looking for dolphins. We would make observations and fill out a data sheet every time we saw a dolphin.

This research has revealed a lot of really interesting information about dolphins: their life span is twice as long as had previously been thought; some of the females in the bay are over fifty years old, while males live somewhat shorter lives.

We were doing our dolphin work out of the Marine Center, and a whale we called Astra happened to be there at that time. She had stranded and the Center was caring for her.

They were seeking volunteers for different shifts; they thought they might be short of people when they did the out-of-water exam. Actually, they never had any trouble finding people to help. I found that kind of a hopeful note about humanity.

Astra is a baby pigmy sperm whale. Needless to say, she is small for a whale, weighing in at a mere 242 pounds. When she lost her mother she ran aground on a beach in southwest Florida.

In human terms, it was a suicide attempt. In Astra's terms, a practical solution to loneliness and the absence of someone to teach her survival basics.

She was saved, however, by the Center's Marine Mammal Rescue Team, and is now swimming around in their tank. She is basically healthy except for a respiratory affliction, perhaps caught from a human. I have a paper mask over my mouth and nose to protect Astra from my germs.

The Center's staff is about to do a medical exam, which involves hauling Astra out of her orphanage with a harness. She has no idea what breaches of privacy and dignity await her; but she has, evidently, her own reasons for joylessness. Chief among these is the lack of other whales.

No one is in the tank feeding Astra, or studying Astra, or playing with Astra at this moment. She swims listlessly, nudging the hula hoops and the innertubes and the balls, finding no interest in any of them. None of them bursts into life and swims away, then back to nudge her in return. She doesn't want a toy; she wants another mammal, preferably a whale.

Companionship at any price is on the way, though. Four people in wet suits are stepping down a ladder into the tank. As the first one enters the water, Astra picks up swimming speed and sharks around the tank in a quick circle.

Her enthusiasm is touchingly transparent. I can't suppress the thought that humans are dubious companionship for one so pure in spirit.

A crane lifts a harnessed Astra out of the tank for her exam. "Watch her tail!" someone says as she clears the rim. A volunteer lifts her tail which looks paper thin and sculpturesque. Eight staff and volunteers hold her and keep her wet by wringing sponges full of water over her while she gets radared, sonared and punctured for blood samples.

We might do well to accept that this is humanity at its best. Consistency is far too much to hope for. People who do a few good things are always being accused of hypocrisy by people who do nothing:

"You wrote a good book, but it's not on recycled paper. You're a hypocrite."

"She changes bedpans in a hospital, but only calls her mother twice a year; she's a hypocrite."

Please, be a hypocrite. The only philosophy possible to live up to is the thinking that you're the only one that matters; anything loftier, discrepancies creep in.

Astra, most likely, will pass her life in captivity. Only loads of both money and luck can change this outcome. She needs a mother. The Center can only give her one if an adult female pigmy sperm whale, one who has borne young, becomes stranded on Florida's shores. If this unlikely event happens, the two whales can be introduced to each other. Then, they can be released into the ocean.

So, probably, Astra will never range freely in the Gulf of Mexico, never find a lifelong travelling companion, never raise young. Her world will be a tank and people will be her friends.

But she will be alive, and she will lift the spirits of many humans.

She will not be a really free pigmy sperm whale, but she will have her own quota of *joie de vivre*, something I believe in my heart all animals possess. No scientist can convince me otherwise. And for this small blessing, the Center's staff and many volunteers give up their evenings and bigger paychecks to keep Astra going.

Hypocrites all, drinking from styrofoam cups, driving oversized vehicles.

I realize I haven't communicated, as I should have by this point, how intense this experience is.

One thing I haven't told you is what Astra looks like. She's button cute, in a way that makes the simple-minded need to take a lot of pictures. She also has the beauty, simplicity, and integrity in which we so often sense we're deficient.

We have some bad moments as she hangs in her harness above the water: someone holding a clipboard says to the vet, "Her inhales and exhales are very short."

A few times she slams her whole body against the floor like an electro-shock patient. A staff member whispers in my ear, "They need to get her back in the water, she's been out almost an hour."

What no one says, but we all feel, is that though there is only the slightest chance Astra could die in this process, we could never really feel the same about ourselves if it were to happen.

But the testing is over now; and the harness, laden with the small whale, swings back over the tank and lowers her to the water.

Safe again, she takes a lap around her pool to be sure of her surroundings.

Hypocrite that I am, I realize with a sudden swell of relief that my face is almost entirely covered by a mask and sunglasses. And if I burst into tears right now, no one will know. ✍

(I called the Marine Center in Florida, in January, 1995, and was told that Astra had died of a systemic infection. It was unknown what caused the infection. Tissues from Astra had been sent off to be examined by researchers who will try to determine more about her illness. - pjf)

Rescues

Physty

Guy D'Angelo became interested in whales as a child, and read all the books he could find on both whales and whaling. It has been a real passion all his life.

Guy has been at the Medical School at Stony Brook University since 1966. He has done research on blood from both beluga whales and dolphins, and discovered a system that previously had been found only in the red blood cells of humans and the higher apes. This system transports glucose very rapidly, moving it from the blood into body cells in under one minute; without this system, under osmotic pressure alone, it takes 1,000 minutes for the same process to take place. Scientists don't know why it is there.

Guy has published two papers about this system, incorporating his love for whales with the research he does.

Physty (pronounced "feisty") was a juvenile sperm whale, maybe four or five years of age, although that's just an estimate. His length was 25 feet, and that we have a pretty good handle on, because of where he was kept for nine days.

He stranded in April, 1981, on the south shore of Long Island, New York. He was lassoed around the base of his tail while he was floundering around beaching himself. Then he was towed backwards, into a boat basin which was not in use at the time in a closed state park, and tied up to a piling. He lay there for the first day, which is when we were notified.

At that time, people who responded to strandings along this coast were a loose-knit group who had an interest in whales; primarily it was a group of students from Bellport High School. Their biology teacher and advisor, Mr. Arthur Cooley, would go along with them. These days, the Okeanos Research Foundation responds to strandings on the Long Island shores.

Previous whales I'd seen and worked with had been dead, but this little guy was alive, and he remained alive. When he was pulled into the boat basin, they put a small net across the mouth of it, keeping him inside. The boat basin was a semicircle and the net closed it off.

The first day, when we heard about it, my wife and I went there right after work. When we saw him, he looked very sick.

People were getting ready to cut him up the next day, because he really looked like a goner. He just lay there. The boat basin was only five feet deep, which I think was what helped to save this whale. He could put his tail on the bottom and lift his blowhole out of the water and take a breath.

That's about all he did the first day. He just lay with his left side facing up and every fifteen or twenty minutes he would lift his head to breathe, so people expected him to die. Well, he didn't.

The next day he was feeling a lot better. They finally cut him loose from the piling so he could swim around that boat basin. The young whale wasn't splashing or anything, but he was exploring the basin.

A fellow named Chris Clark was very interested in the sounds of whales. He had been with Roger Payne in South America, in Patagonia, and also been in Point Barrow, Alaska. Chris devised a system of three underwater microphones. By receiving signals in this triangular array of microphones, he could tell where the animal was and thus accurately locate the position of the animal. Chris came down the second or third night to record the sperm whale; if the animal was, indeed, making sounds. I have a copy of the tape he made. The whale was feeling a lot better, making many clicking sounds all around the place.

About the third or fourth day a group arrived from a small diving museum in City Island, in the Bronx. It was run by Mike Sandlofer, an ex-Navy diver. He has an excellent museum of ancient diving equipment, all kinds of neat things. Now there is a large display about Physty, as this whale was nicknamed.

When Mike got into the water with Physty, he was the first person to touch the whale in a friendly sort of way. He fed him squid that was loaded with chlorim-phenicol. They felt he had pneumonia and that this was the most potent antibiotic they could give a whale.

The first time he gave Physty squid, Mike just had a snorkel on, no tank. It was early evening, around sunset. While he was feeding Physty, Mike's hand was in the whale's mouth. Mike was talking to us: "I feel him turning the squid around with his tongue, so he has the head first. He'll swallow the legs last. I can feel him doing that..."

All of a sudden Mike disappeared under the water. Oh boy...everyone was standing there looking at each other, wondering what happened and not knowing what to do.

Two minutes later, poof! Mike came up with a big grin.

"Well," he said, "he let me go!"

Physty had grabbed Mike's arm, clamped down onto it and took him underwater. Mike started to struggle, and hit him a few times on the side of his head. Physty must have realized what he was doing, because he opened his mouth and Mike was free to come back to the surface. Mike continued to feed Physty daily until his release on the ninth day, and the whale never did that again.

Samples of Physty's blood as well as tissue from around his blowhole were taken. They could not find any causative agent for his illness; at least, not in the range of tests they looked at. Obviously he was very sick, but he was getting better.

Of course, this all attracted great crowds of people. Our group, along with some of the other groups, served as crowd control in a unique way. Rather than in a police type of way, each volunteer was assigned to be with an unarmed, plainclothes park ranger. We had ropes all around the basin so people wouldn't fall in the water. We would tell people, "If you want your questions answered about this whale, please stay behind the ropes. Don't yell and don't holler." This worked very well. We had thousands of people come to see him, including bus loads of school children. We kept them quiet and orderly just by answering their questions.

About the third or fourth day, we could see that Physty was feeling a heck of a lot better. Swimming around the boat basin at ease, he could have left anytime he wanted to. The net stretched across the opening was one of those nets people use to catch baitfish; a little seine net with floats on it. I'm sure he could have swum right through it.

I think he realized that he was safe here. He was getting fed, maybe not a tenth of his normal diet, but something with medicine in it. He was now able to keep his head above water and breathe. After the fourth day, he could swim upright, and he no longer lay on his side.

Over the Easter weekend in early April, on Easter Sunday to be exact, my wife and I arrived in the mid-afternoon to relieve the people who had worked that morning. Again, we were serving both as crowd control and information people. I was standing on the dock with the park ranger next to me.

All of a sudden, the ranger started to poke me and pull on my sleeve. I had been facing the crowd answering questions, so I turned towards the ranger, and asked, "What's the matter?" He didn't say anything, he just pointed towards the water.

There was Physty. He had swum between the pier posts and his head was right up against the dock at our feet. That's how we got a good measurement of his length: it was 25 feet from the pier post to the dock. His tail was by the post and his head was by the dock.

The ranger asked, "What are we supposed to do?"

I just said, "Bend down and pet him."

It was obvious that Physty was curious. The ranger bent down and patted him by his blowhole, and Physty stayed there for a few minutes before slowly swimming back to the middle of the basin.

Until then Physty had avoided contact with people who were standing on the dock. This time he had swum in and initiated the contact and was not threatened by that contact at all. From then on he was more active. During the day he would mostly log around, sleeping or being lazy. In the evenings he would come to life; actively swimming and click-training the pier posts and everything in the basin with his "sonar."

His clicks were just unbelievable. When you were standing on this solid wooden dock, or bulkhead filled with dirt, there was no air space between you and the water. When Physty clicked in your direction, you could actually feel the vibration of his clicks coming up through the soles of your shoes.

One cold evening we were standing on the dock. People were stamping their feet to keep warm, and all of a sudden Physty is answering their stamps. He was mimicking what they were stamping, with his clicks.

My wife picked this up and started playing a little game with him, stamping in sequences. He would mimic stamps up to five beats. In other words; you could do 2-3, 4-1, any combination up to five beats. and he would repeat it accurately. After five beats he would give you a very BR-BR-BR-BR-BR-BR-BR-BR click-train, as if to say, "I don't want to play this game this way. Give me five beats."

We remembered this for years. I believe the January, 1993 issue of the *Journal for Marine Mammalogy* published data about sperm whale codas. The data had been collected in both the South Pacific and the South Atlantic in 1981; I think it is interesting that it wasn't published until 1993. Over 50% of the transmissions of these whales were five-beat codas. They were identifying themselves, like tribal identification, with a five-beat coda.

So what Physty must have been doing is trying to find out what our coda was. We were probably confusing him no end, because we changed our beat rhythm all the time. He kept repeating whatever we stamped, but we kept changing what we stamped. He was trying to find out what tribe or pod we belonged to, but he never got the same answer twice.

Towards the end of his stay, perhaps on the sixth day, he was really OK. We all knew he was healthy again, because he was swimming a lot, playing games, and letting people touch him. He'd play this little game: he'd swim in and you'd touch him, then he'd swim five or six inches away to see if you could touch him again. He would just get to the point where you couldn't reach him. The students would sit on each other's legs and try to figure out all sorts of acrobatic ways of extending their reach a few more inches to touch him. He was training us to do tricks for him.

He played another game one particular evening which we called the "sailing game." He would pick his tail up out of the water, literally, and use it as a sail. He would usually swim to the middle of the basin, pick his tail up, catch the wind, and let the wind carry him to the edge of the boat basin. When he felt the edge, he would start the game all over again.

One evening he was playing this game. Everyone else was feeling rather chilled, so they went off to a heated trailer which the Long Island Beach Buggy Association brought to the park for our use. With a stove, it was great for getting out of the wind and cold. I was not cold, so I stayed to watch Physty.

I was alone with the whale. The other people were not yet to the trailer, but I knew if I yelled to get their attention he would swim away. He did not like loud sounds or bright lights. He really got frightened one night when a film crew from one of the local TV stations came down to film in the middle of the night and turned on their floodlights. He really got upset. I was ready to throw the cameraman into the water because I told them not to turn on their bright lights, and they did it anyway.

That evening there was a strong wind blowing, and Physty sailed downwind into the corner of the boat basin where I was standing. I knelt down and I patted him on the top of his head, pretty close to his blowhole, because that was the only part of the whale out of the water.

Physty had obviously put his tail on the bottom; that's the only way he could have done this: he proceeded to slowly, and I mean very slowly, lift his whole head out of the water in front of me.

Within 30 or 40 seconds I was faced with this huge head! Of course, I couldn't see very much because it was quite dark. But I could see the outline of it, towering above me.

Then he started to click-train me. Very rapid BR-BR-BR-BR-BR-BR-BR-BR-BR-BR-BR-BR-BR-BR-BR-BR-BR-BR- BR-BR-BR-BR-BR! Just like that. It was like standing in front of a big woofer speaker. I could feel the higher pitched sounds going up and down my body. I was kneeling so it started at my knees going through my torso, lung area and up to my head.

Meanwhile, I was petting him all around, feeling this huge bulbous nose. I reached around and felt the indentations underneath his upper jaw, the sockets where his teeth would eventually grow. I felt his lower jaw and the little teeth buds on the very tip of the jaw. He just had little budding teeth.

All the while I was talking to him. "Hello, how are you? How ya doing? What 'cha doing, boy?"

I put my hand on the notch where his head curved in a little bit and then curved out again to form the top of the upper jaw. And right in the notch was the focal point of the sound. That's where the "monkey's fist" is located, as the old whalers used to call it: the valve that's underneath the blowhole, where the two airways meet just before going out to the single blowhole. That's where they merge, and that's where the cartilaginous plate is. And, that's where he produces the sound. It was obvious, by putting my hand right there, that was where the sound was most intense.

We stood there together for at least three minutes. Both exploring one another: me with my hand, and my eyes as best I could in the dark; and him, of course, with his sonications.

During this time, the whole time, he did not stop. It was a continual BR-BR-BR-BR-BR-BR-BR-BR-BR-BR-BR-BR-BR-BR-BR! I could feel it sweeping up and down my body. He was focusing on me, going down and up, and down and up, from head to toe and back. We just stood there for quite a while. Then, I guess, he got tired. Very slowly, as if to say, "There's nothing to be afraid of, I'm not going to hurt you," he sank back down into the water again.

At that point I got up and ran to the trailer to tell everybody else. They all came running out to see if something like this would happen again, or at least to see if they could pet him again. But he stayed away from people for the rest of that night.

This event really changed my view of animal life. If nothing else, although I was convinced before this, I truly believe that we are dealing with an extremely high level of intelligence in whales. There is no doubt in my mind that they are on a level with us.

He was young, a teenager, I suppose, and here he was, dragged in from the ocean, in a most unceremonious manner. Close to death, probably scared stiff. And now, within a few days, he realized there is nothing here to hurt him, and he is trying to make contact with us.

On the ninth day, they lowered the net and brought in a little Zodiac and shooed Physty out of the boat basin. He headed right for sea and was followed by a small flotilla of Coast Guard vessels. Physty disappeared into the ocean when he got three or four miles out. There is a white circle around the base of his tail where the rope burned into his skin when they towed him into the boat basin, so he's marked for life and easy to recognize.

Physty has been seen since he was released, swimming out there in the Atlantic Ocean with his pod. He's found them. ◁

Fin Whale In England

*Nick Tregenza is a British doctor who has been interested in ceta-
ceans for quite some time, and has done several research projects
on them. One project involved interviewing a thousand people
about what they have seen in the ocean over the years: sightings
of whales or dolphins, as well as water spouts, basking sharks,
and Portuguese Man-of-War. This study produced some fascinating stories as well as a remarkably clear and particularly unex-
pected picture of the changes that have taken place in the ocean.*

*One story which emerged was of regular sightings of dol-
phins driving schools of fish into a muddy tidal shallows called
Hooe Lake, near Plymouth. The dolphins never entered the lake,
but waited in the entrance channel until the falling tide forced
the fish out, down the narrow channel, and into the mouths of
the scheming dolphins. No one had seen this for 40 years. When
the researchers looked at the navigational chart for the estuary,
they found that the water outside Hooe Lake was named "Dolphin Pond."*

Somebody rang me on the phone about a whale that was
stranded a couple of miles from where I live in Penzance, Cornwall.
I happened to have the United Kingdom's Sea-Watching Guru
staying with me at the time, so we went over and had a look.

There was a young fin whale rolling in the water upside down
in a gully. There was a lot of blood in the water; it was horrible.
We thought the whale was dying. We looked at it for a while and
thought, "We can't bear to watch this," and left. The whale was
head first in a rocky gully and obviously could not get out.

Later in the day a television crew came by my home and asked
me to come with them to tell them about the whale. When we got
to the gully again, we with saw that the whale was exactly as it had
been in the morning, except that the tide had come in a bit further.

A man turned up who had actually seen the whale come into
this gully. He said the whale had come in over the rock at the
entrance, on a big surging wave. Then the tide had gone down
and trapped it.

When the tide rose again the whale still could not get out. It
had no reverse gear, and there was no room for it to turn around.

Clearly the whale was not dying, as it was still moving around in the same sort of way as in the morning. Several men from a nearby lifeboat station arrived on the scene. It looked too dangerous for anyone to get in among the rocks with the whale rolling around, so we hatched a plan of getting a rope around the whale's tail without going into the water.

With a man on the outermost rocks on either side of the gully, we waited for the whale to lift its tail. When it did, we flicked the rope underneath. It worked the first time.

We then brought the two ends shoreward ahead of the whale and crossed them over three times. We then moved the two ends apart, so the crossings moved down towards the tail and tightened up a bit on the tail stock. When the rope got tight the whale gave a visible shudder, which was really surprising to us. Although it was bashing against the rocks at times, we hadn't seen it move like that. The shudder seemed to be in response to our tightening the rope around its tail.

We then put ten people on the rope and pulled the whale's tail around sideways to try and turn it, using a bit of space on one side of the gully. The whale started wallowing vertically as if to assist us. Gradually it did turn around and began swimming. It made it over the rock and was in deep water again.

We worried that it would probably swim straight out to sea trailing two hundred feet of rope. But no, the whale stopped. We untwisted the rope exactly the same number of times as we had twisted it, and let one end go. The whale slowly swam out. It seemed to have waited for us to untwist the rope.

By this time the light was fading, and a great cheer went up as we saw it swim freely. The whale slowly turned left towards the shallow water of Mounts Bay; we were filled with fear that it might strand again. But after a couple of hundred yards, it turned seawards and started to move more strongly, rising higher to breathe.

We never saw that whale again.

Talking about it later, we agreed that the whale had some sort of feelings that it was being helped and was trying to assist us. Maybe this is projection on our part, but that is what it seemed like.

Fin whales are not common in our waters, but every year there are a few reported by local fishermen and sea watchers. ✍

Baleen Whale in the Virgin Islands

Henry Tonnemacher *has lived in the Caribbean for over 20 years, since he graduated from college. Henry came to St. Croix to direct the diving program for Farleigh-Dickenson University's Marine Lab. He was involved in setting up the "Hydro-Lab," a habitat where scientists lived in a chamber underwater for a week at a time, which Henry has done four times himself. The purpose of this chamber is that a diver can stay at 100 feet for six hours rather than 30 minutes, as when diving from the surface. Teams of divers live in the chamber at 100 feet for a week at a time, doing long time deep water dives. At the end of the week they decompress very slowly, taking all day to reach the surface in the chamber. The chamber was later put on display in the Smithsonian Institution.*

Henry had a 40-foot trimaran until Hurricane Hugo flipped it over when the eye of the storm came through. He was aboard his boat, anchored in a theoretically safe spot on the south side of St. Croix, but the boat was totally destroyed, along with everything he owned. Henry says that he got to start life over again.

This particular incident was with either a fin, sei, or minke whale. It was a baleen whale, about 25 feet long.

I was doing environmental work on St. Croix in the Virgin Islands. I saw a huge amount of splashing out on Long Reef, the barrier reef protecting Christiansted Harbor. At first I thought fish were feeding, but then I could see tremendous splashing and realized it was something extremely large.

I jumped into my dinghy and sped to the outside of the reef, where I saw a whale trapped on the inside of the reef. The whale's head was pointing due north, perpendicular to the reef.

Perhaps he was thinking this would be the only way he could get back to the ocean, because that appeared to be the way the whale had come into the harbor. I could see the path of broken coral in the reef he made on his way in. The tide had dropped and there was no way the whale could have gotten back out over the reef.

The ocean's swells were really big that day; the whale must have been too close to the reef and was washed over it. The water is very deep on the Atlantic side of the reef.

My initial reaction was that the whale was sick or injured. Something must be seriously wrong with this animal for him to have been washed over the reef. When I looked more closely at the whale, I could see many cuts and abrasions on him, but none that looked really bad.

I came back inside the reef, anchored the dinghy nearby, got into the water with snorkeling gear, and swam to the whale. I touched him first over his eye, stroking this big, trapped animal like I was petting a cat. I hoped to get the idea across that I was there to help him and not harm him in any way.

There was a hundred yards of shallow water with small head corals and sea grass between the whale and the deep water channel into the harbor. The water by the whale was about four feet deep. He was barely buoyant, scraping his belly on the bottom. All I could think of was to get the whale into the ship channel a hundred yards away.

I began to push his nose and his head towards the east, the direction he needed to go. I would push on his head, then swim back and pull on one of his pectoral fins. I repeated this pushing and pulling for 15 to 20 minutes and was actually able to turn the whale 90 degrees. He now pointed in the direction of the deep water.

I began to push from behind his pectoral fin, then swam out in front of the whale. I would come back and push again, then swim in front of him. I repeated this pushing and swimming in front of him many times.

Amazingly enough, it seemed as though he understood that I wanted him to go in that direction. He began to swim, slowly pumping his tail fluke up and down. And so, by pushing, prodding and swimming in front of him, I got the whale to follow me through the hundred yards of shallow water to the ship channel.

What really amazed me is that once the whale got into deep water, he seemed to know exactly what to do. He could easily have gone to the south and been hopelessly trapped in the harbor, which is pretty big with many shallow areas. Instead, he continued to swim to the east, then followed the dog-leg the channel made to the northwest. He was soon in the Atlantic Ocean, swimming freely. The whale took several breaths at the surface and was gone.

It was an amazing experience being in the water with this animal, literally eye-to-eye with him. He had to know that I was trying to help him; I can't otherwise explain how he knew what to do once he was pointed in the right direction.

It is a nice feeling to think that I might have saved this whale's life. I feel fortunate to have been in the right place at the right time, and that my ideas of how to help the whale worked. ⨞

Blue Whale in Nova Scotia

Sean Todd belongs to the Whale Research Group in Newfoundland, Canada. He is studying trophic and foraging relationships in humpback whales as part of his PhD program.

One important function of the Group is to help fishermen release whales, usually humpbacks, tangled in fishing gear. It is an exhausting but exhilarating experience, often requiring direct contact from a tiny rubber inflatable boat with a 35-foot long leviathan. Armed only with hooked knives to cut the nets, the Group, led by Jon Lien, has endeavored to both minimize costs to fishermen and save whales.

Much of the research the Whale Research Group does is centered around entrapment, its causes and how to prevent it. However, they also get involved in a number of related investigations.

In the fall of 1992, we received a call that a whale, probably a humpback, was attempting to beach itself in a bay approximately two hundred miles north of our lab in St. John's. At the time I was also involved in a project to take electrocardiograms (EKG) of humpbacks, and such a stranding represented an ideal opportunity.

Once at the site, we found the whale in a small shallow cove, facing towards us. It would take a breath (blow) every minute or so. We immediately realized this was not a humpback whale. The whale was approximately 50 feet long, thin and torpedo-shaped, and had a blue-grey shade to its skin. It was a blue whale.

This was exciting to us, as an EKG from a blue whale would be extremely valuable data. The blue whale is the largest creature ever to live; it has the largest heart of all creatures living on earth today.

It was difficult to figure out why this animal had stranded. It had lost its dorsal fin, most likely in some collision with a propeller; we could see a propeller's concentric scrapes on the whale's back. But its present difficulties were not because of injuries sustained during its dorsal fin accident, as that had obviously healed over some time ago.

It was a reasonably young individual. Various blood tests we performed later suggested that there may have been some kind of infection, but our understanding of whale health is still very limited.

The whale had swum into the end of an L-shaped bay, moving progressively into more shallow water. Eventually it had grounded on the beach, facing into the land, half submerged by water. To complicate matters, the tide was starting to recede. In five hours, the whale would be almost completely out of the water. In such large animals this is highly dangerous as the animal's own weight, once out of the supporting water, will crush many of its internal organs, including the lungs.

At any stranding, the first job is to assess the situation and determine possible solutions to the problem. While trying to figure out how to turn this gargantuan whale around to face outwards towards the ocean, blood samples were taken. We also measured the animal's EKG, using suction cup electrodes attached to a recorder.

About this time the media turned up, and the crowds got thicker. Often half the job at stranding events is trying to handle the public attention. While we know they are concerned and want to help, the sheer number of people can often push the animal into a state of panic.

Finally a game plan emerged. A few of us, including a local vet, put on dry suits and launched our small inflatable. We thought that the best thing to do was to get the whale to turn around on its own. Given the weight of the animal, around 30 tons, we could never hope to move it ourselves. All we could do was encourage the whale to turn in the correct direction.

So we used some planks and long oars and tried to prod the whale into a direction facing away from the beach. Six of us took positions along the length of the whale and began to push on it. I was by its mouth.

Of course the whale did not like this new sensation. This was part of our plan; in an effort to get away from us, the whale would eventually shrug itself off the bank and face out into the bay. For safety purposes, we were ready to leap back at a moment's notice; the animal still had a degree of mobility and could easily hurt us.

While the whale obviously did not enjoy being manhandled, we had to accept the fact that we had to be "cruel to be kind." It was up to us to get this whale turned around, or it would end up dying on dry land.

Over the course of an hour and a half we got the whale turned 90 degrees. The animal always seemed to want to turn back into the shore, but we kept pushing it around. Eventually we managed to move it a full 180 degrees. It was right at the end of this turn when disaster struck. As I was levering the mouth across, the oar I was using snapped. The whale, likely sensing there was no more resistance by its mouth, started to move back into shore towards me.

By this time, we were all very tense. I glanced back and forth between my broken oar and the approaching mouth of this huge whale. I immediately realized that I was about to see one and a half hour's work, very sweaty work, go down the drain, and I had no way to stop it. I also knew that the opportunity to move the whale off the sand bank was diminishing as the tide got lower and lower. For some reason I saw red; I had five other volunteers depending on me to keep the whale from moving back, so I literally did something very, very stupid: I stuck my leg in the way.

It was only that night, when I got to bed and couldn't sleep, that I realized what a dangerous thing I had done. The whale, if it had wanted to, would have just gone straight over me, crushing me like a bug.

But it didn't. The whale stopped against my leg and didn't move any farther. Perhaps it thought it was the oar again or some equivalent that it couldn't push against. It just rested its head against my leg. At which time I said, in as calm a voice as I could manage, "Ah, guys, I could really do with another oar here!" I certainly didn't want my leg to stay there forever.

Another oar arrived quickly and replaced my leg. We finally were able to complete the full 180-degree turn. The whale still continued to react, its mouth opening every now and again as it tried to readjust itself. Being by the mouth, I'd see this huge gullet opening in front of me; quite an exciting and intimidating experience.

Now I know how Jonah felt!

Once the whale was turned around, we slid a rope around its tail and pulled it up behind the pectoral fins in a loop around its body. We then attached the rope to several fishing boats waiting offshore. The combination of the boats pulling and us irritating the whale finally got it off the beach and into deeper water.

As soon as the whale was swimming freely we transferred the "reins" of our bridle to our inflatable, and we began to move out of the bay. After a few minutes the whale began to swim rather than be towed, and started to move ahead of us. Eventually the whale was towing us, rather than vice-versa.

Now I knew how the Basque whalers felt once they had harpooned a whale and were dragged along; the original Nantucket sleigh ride! It was clear now the whale was quite capable of swimming on its own, so we cut the rope and pulled it away. Off the whale went, out of the bay.

As we watched the whale disappear into the distance, we realized, to our dismay, that it was traveling in an exact straight line in the last direction that we pointed it.

The whale headed straight across to the other side of the bay, where it grounded again!

This time the whale grounded in much deeper water, so we couldn't get out of the boat to help it. But the noise from the motor persuaded it to move off the bank again. Once more the whale swam across the bay, only to ground on another sand bank on the same side of the bay as the original stranding. We figured out the animal's orientation system; it headed in whatever direction it was last pointed.

Once we realized this, we knew we were going to have to accompany the whale all the way out to sea. Because the bay was L-shaped, and we were still in the lower part of that L, we would at some point have to turn the whale around a headland. We began a new strategy, keeping alongside the animal so that it steered correctly. Once off the last sand bank, it began to speed up and start to blow more regularly. It was a wonderful sight. Blue whales cut through the water much more gracefully than humpbacks.

Unfortunately, the whale was soon swimming too fast for us to keep up with, given our low-powered engine and the number of people in our boat. The whale charged on, heading for the corner of the bay. There was a harbor there, which the whale went straight into. On the quayside were two young kids with homemade fishing poles fishing for crabs. The whale went right past them, just below their feet!

The whale became stuck yet again in the shallow depths of the harbor, rolled on its side, and began to open and close its gaping mouth. Quickly afterwards our boat, full of divers, buzzed in after the whale and began pushing it out of the harbor.

All of this took place within 30 seconds or so. I'm sure no one believed these goggle-eyed kids the next day at show-and-tell in school. But certainly they know exactly what a blue whale's tonsils look like, if they have them.

As last we maneuvered the whale to the open ocean. Off it went. That was the last we saw of our young blue whale.

As a postscript to this tale, we got home that night to find the story on the local TV channels. They showed bits of film of us turning the whale around, and also of us applying the suction cup that housed the EKG electrode. Unfortunately, the reporter never had a chance to talk to us about what we were doing. Instead, their imaginative explanation for that particular piece of footage was that we were applying electrical stimulation to provoke the whale into a reaction. As if we were trying to defibrillate the whale's heart!

I don't think they realized that if we had been applying electrical current to the whale, we certainly would not have wanted to be in the salt water with it! ⊰

Sean Todd dedicated the retelling of this tale to the people who helped rescue the whale.

Pilot Whales In Tasmania

Peter Brand was born and raised in Tasmania, the island state in the southeast corner of Australia. He met his Canadian wife Penny in 1972, while they were exploring northern Australia. They teamed up to travel overland through Asia and Africa, a journey which ultimately took them to over sixty countries around the world before they eventually settled on the Saanich Peninsula near Victoria, British Columbia.

Penny is an operating room nurse and Peter teaches 7th and 8th grades in a Native school.

In July, 1989, our family had the good fortune to spearhead the rescue of several pilot whales after they stranded on two remote beaches in Tasmania. At the time, our sons Josh and Aidan were 6 and 4 years old.

We were visiting with my mother Joan Brand at her small seaside resort located on the Freycinet Peninsula on Tasmania's east coast. I was sweeping the front steps when I heard a very loud hissing and blowing from the bay.

Looking down from the patio, I was astonished to see a pod of approximately eighty pilot whales in what I thought to be a feeding frenzy. I rushed to get our video camera and called to the family to come see the spectacle. Our observation site was ten feet above sea level and about 70 yards from the corner of Coles Bay where the whales were located.

We were convinced that the whales were feeding, as a large school of dolphins had entered the bay that morning, feeding on squid.

As we watched and videotaped the pilot whales, they swam into ever shallower water until the leaders ran aground and began thrashing and rolling, frantically trying to extricate themselves from this death trap. (We were to learn later that our videotape was the first known recording of pre-stranding behavior and a stranding in progress.)

The sounds rising from the beach added to the drama of the moment. Rolling and thrashing, the distressed mammals whipped the shallow water to foam, accompanied by much hissing, blowing, squeaks and squeals.

We rushed down the narrow trail to the white sand beach and found five whales stranded. A big male, whom I assumed was the leader of the pod, stationed himself in water about four feet deep, with his pectoral fins resting on the sandy ocean floor and his back breaking the surface. The rest of the pod retreated about 100 yards offshore, where they cruised in a tight circle.

The closest of the stranded whales was now resting quietly in the shallows at the water's edge, occasionally giving a forlorn flap of its tail. It rolled to one side, eying us nervously; then it opened its mouth to expose a row of evenly spaced inch-long white teeth.

Knowing nothing of the habits or attitudes of stranded pilot whales towards would-be human rescuers, I was at first wary of the large teeth and tail. I approached rather as I would a nervous horse, talking gently and reaching out to stroke the smooth black skin. The tail flopped again disconsolately, rather like the friendly tail-flop of a large dog.

I felt this meant that the whale intended me no harm and approached the head more confidently, stroking, talking, and splashing water over the eyes to wash away the sand which had gathered there.

Looking around for help I noticed that apart from my family the beach was practically deserted. A small group of Japanese tourists was snapping pictures from a safe distance. A young couple spending their honeymoon at my mother's resort were the only other people at the scene. I asked Greg, the newlywed, if he would help me try to get the whale into deeper water. Fortunately the whale had ended its struggle facing out to sea. It was a very calm evening, with hardly a ripple on the water, save those created by the rest of the pod which was still circling patiently offshore. Thankfully the tide was rising.

Stripped to our underwear, we took a firm grip at the back of the pectoral fins as we strained to pull the six-foot long body seaward. At first, our efforts seemed futile, but then, almost imperceptibly, the sleek black mammal began inching toward deeper water. As its belly came free of the sand, it gave a couple of deft strokes of its tail and glided out to rejoin the pod.

The four other whales had all managed to free themselves, leaving the large lone male still holding his station thirty yards offshore. I waded out to him to check that he wasn't stranded and as I reached out to touch him, he gave a gentle flick of his tail and cruised back to the pod.

About this time my friend Mike Dicker, who operated the local school bus, arrived at the end of his evening run, just as the whales were reunited. I suggested rowing out to them to attempt to shepherd them back towards open water. Mike agreed; he is an experienced diver and had shown me his collection of photographs he had taken while swimming with gray whales on their annual migration north through the Tasman Sea.

Josh and I quickly donned our wet suits and snorkeling gear while Mike grabbed his camera from his bus. As a freelance photographer for *The Examiner* newspaper, he always has his camera handy.

Josh, Mike, and I piled into a ten-foot aluminium dinghy and rowed out toward the pod of whales, still circling a couple of hundred yards offshore. By this time the sun was setting across ten-mile wide Great Oyster Bay; the red, orange and golden hues reflected in the calm water. I videotaped the pod circling against

a backdrop formed by The Hazards, a magnificent red granite mountain range which turns a stunning pink as the sun sets.

I turned to Mike and asked, "Do you think it would be safe to swim with the whales?"

"Absolutely!" said Mike, without a doubt. A little apprehensive at first, I gently slipped into the water. "Can I come too?" asked Josh excitedly. "Just let me check things out first," I replied.

I swam towards the pod and watched in awe as they glided through the water just feet below me. It soon became apparent that they did not mind our swimming with them, so I returned to the dinghy for Josh. Mike picked up the video camera and began taping as we swam toward the pod of whales still lolling in the sunset.

I intended to keep to the outside of the pod, but in minutes we were completely surrounded by them. We noticed that as the whales swam beneath us, they would lower their tails, seemingly to avoid hitting us, then as they passed clear of us they would resume their normal swimming position.

Josh and I remained in company with the whales for about fifteen minutes, enthralled by their gentleness toward us and each other. We estimated the pod to number approximately eighty, and even when swimming in close company there appeared to be no bumping or jostling. The whales allowed us to approach so close that we could reach out and touch them as they passed beneath us.

For a father and his six-year-old son, swimming hand in hand, this was to be a shared moment of communion with nature which we shall never forget.

By a typically Tasmanian coincidence, our dinner guests that evening were Rod and Marguerite Scott. Rod is the editor of *The Examiner*, and had arrived in time to watch Josh, Mike, and me swimming with the whales. The story appeared in the paper the next morning, where it was spotted by the News Editor of the Tasmanian Public Television Channel of ABC-TV. When the editor phoned for details and heard that we had captured the whole story on video tape, the news anchorman chartered a helicopter and flew up to see us in the hope that they could use our tape.

After they arrived and copied our tape, Josh and I were invited to join the news crew aboard the helicopter to see if we could find the whales. We were alarmed to see them just a couple of miles away and again very close to a remote beach.

The helicopter then returned us to our home before flying back to the city for the newsmen to file their story. That evening the dramatic footage of the stranding, rescue, and our swim with the whales was beamed around Australia. As we watched the footage shot from the helicopter on the television news story, Rod Scott, Mike Dicker, and I expressed our alarm at how close the whales seemed to be to the shore. We decided to take Rod's 16-foot power boat around the coast the next morning to look for the whales.

At mid-morning the next day we found the whales about four miles from the site of the original stranding.

Five whales had stranded on sandy, gently shallowing Cook's Beach. Once again, the tide was rising, but a chill midwinter wind was blowing onto the beach with a fairly heavy chop. The waves broke on the beach and over the whales, filling their eyes with sand. Again, the rest of the pod was stationed about a quarter of a mile out to sea, milling about in one area.

After getting ashore with our equipment and anchoring the boat in deeper water, we radioed a message to the National Park Ranger at Coles Bay, telling him that we had found the whales and suggesting that we might need help with a rescue. We then inspected the stranded whales.

All of them lay on their sides with one pectoral fin buried in the sand. Of the five animals, two were dead.

The three live whales occasionally flopped their tails hopelessly. They opened their eyes to look at us, then closed them again to keep out the sand being flung on them by the waves. They breathed with a loud and rhythmic blow and gasp, a short sharp exhale followed by a longer inhale.

The breathing of the whales and the breaking waves was to be our accompaniment for the next three hours as we struggled to save the whales.

The three whales measured about ten feet, twelve feet and eighteen feet long. They had stranded on a rising tide and the waves had washed them parallel to the beach, with their pectoral fins almost completely buried. The wave action had created a hump of sand on their seaward side and a hollow on their shore side, similar to a stranded log.

We began with the smallest whale, which offered the best chance of success. At first, we pivoted it around so that its head was facing out to sea. We tried to pull it towards deeper water by its pectoral fins. This was the method which had worked well at the first stranding, but this time we faced several factors which combined to make the task more difficult.

With one man straining at each pectoral fin and the third pushing at the tail we couldn't budge the whale an inch.

Moreover, we soon noticed that we had broken the smooth black skin behind the whale's pectoral fins. We were surprised at how delicate the skin was and decided to abandon this method and find some other way to move the whale.

People have since asked why we didn't hitch a rope onto the whales and use the boat to tow them off the beach. One only needs to plant a small anchor on the beach and try to pull against it so see how futile this is. The boat's propeller simply whips the water to foam without any headway. The dead weight of even the smallest whale was ten times more resistant than any anchor.

Imagine, also, trying to drag a plastic bag full of cement, weighing perhaps three hundred pounds, across a wet sandy beach without damaging the bag. This was something like the predicament we found ourselves in, except that we were dealing with a beautiful, living, breathing mammal.

Between concerted efforts to heave the whale towards the water, we would stop to rest and calm the poor creature. We did this by stroking its head, talking calmly and washing the sand away from the eyes and breathing hole. The whale continued to breathe steadily and give the occasional futile flop of its tail.

We knew that a great danger to all three live whales was that their own body weight would eventually crush their lungs and cause them to suffocate. We also knew that their skin should not be allowed to dry out, so we constantly washed them down.

Having damaged the skin with our head-first pulling method, we decided to try turning the whale around and pulling tail first. This would certainly give us something decent to hang onto, but we were concerned that the pectoral fins would dig into the sand, acting like brakes and possibly injuring the whale. We again dragged the whale around, turning it 180 degrees.

Even this seemingly simple task took about fifteen minutes, with rest stops for us and the whale, plus digging by hand to ensure that the pectoral fins remained free of the ever-clutching sand. Periodically one of us would pick up the cameras to record progress both on film and video.

Once turned around, we stationed one man on the tail and one at each pectoral fin, lifting and pushing the head and fins. Finally we felt the whale begin to move seaward, slowly at first, then gaining speed as our adrenaline pumped and the water grew deeper. Once sure that the whale was clear, I rushed for the video camera and recorded the last few moments of its once-in-a-lifetime journey in reverse, the whale's black body escorted by two wet suited rescuers.

Floating at last and sensing the ocean on all sides, the whale gave a few powerful strokes of its tail and headed straight towards the pod, still waiting patiently offshore.

Rod and Mike cheered and clapped. Rod yelled, "We got one off! We got one off!" and thrust his fist in the air. We were all elated as we watched the dorsal fin head purposefully out to sea.

Energized by our success, we immediately went to inspect the two other live whales. They were both still breathing steadily. We selected the smaller of the two and adopted the new rescue method immediately.

We got this whale afloat quite quickly, motivated by a combination of confidence and haste born out of our fear for the whales' safety the longer they remained stranded. Freed, the second whale also turned immediately in the direction of the pod and made a beeline away from us, without stopping to say thanks!

We now turned our attention to the third whale. We were obviously running on adrenaline, having been engaged in heavy physical work for several hours with nothing to eat or drink. None of us seemed to notice.

The last whale presented the greatest challenge. The biggest of the three, it was about eighteen feet long and must have weighed over a thousand pounds.

At first the task seemed daunting. We tried the technique which had brought us success previously. One inch at a time, we turned the huge body until its tail was toward the sea. This was much heavier going than the other two and we had to stop more often to take a breather. (At the time I had a hernia in need of repair and this exercise certainly wasn't doing it any good!) At each break we would stroke the whale's head, bathe it with water, and clean the sand from its eyes.

The heaving and straining dragged on for nearly an hour. Periodically we would cast a hopeful look to the west to see if help was on the way. At last, one such glance revealed two boats speeding toward us. In minutes the ranger and a half-dozen volunteers arrived at the scene. They quickly joined us heaving on the exhausted whale.

The extra manpower worked wonders. In a couple of minutes we had the whale in chest-high water. We supported it there while it slowly regained the feeling in its body and fins.

Then this whale, too, turned in the direction of the pod and swam slowly seaward, leaning slightly over to one side. Mike, a lifeguard and very strong swimmer, accompanied the whale for a hundred yards or so, then stopped and watched it go out of sight. I recorded the whale's swim to freedom on videotape.

We quickly gathered up our belongings and followed the last of the rescued whales back towards the pod in our boats. By the time we caught up, it was swimming very strongly. A large school of dolphins was frolicking around the pod, adding an air of celebration to the scene.

Penny, Josh, and Aidan arrived with a flotilla of boats which had come out from Coles Bay. Mike, Rod, and I decided to swim with the pod. Again, I invited Josh to join us.

We hoped to spot the whales we had rescued. We were able to identify them by wounds on their skin left by cookie cutter sharks. As their name implies, these predators leave a hole the size and shape of a cookie in the skin of their prey. The wounds don't seem to bother the victims too much and heal over in time, leaving distinctive scars.

We donned our snorkeling gear and plunged into the water, joining the whales and dolphins. Rod was the first one in, and I videotaped him as he was greeted by the last whale we had rescued. Rod hitched a ride on the big whale's dorsal fin as it swam by. The whale did not seem to mind.

Again Josh and I had the thrill of a lifetime, swimming hand in hand with the pod. As they passed under us they would roll to one side and peer up at us.

The images of this incredible experience will be imprinted in our memories forever. It seemed that for a time we and the whales accompanied each other in some kind of suspended animation. We all seemed to be swimming in slow motion, enjoying each other's company. We noticed that the small young whales were always escorted by two adults, one at each side.

Then a really thrilling thing happened. The big whale we had worked so long and hard to free swam over to me. It cruised by at arm's length, enabling me to reach out and stroke its sleek side. It was clearly identifiable by a distinctive shark bite on its back, which we had examined closely while it lay on the beach. Rod and Mike also received a visit from this whale.

We all felt this was its way of thanking us for freeing them.

That afternoon a storm began to brew, scattering the flotilla of small craft which had come out to join in the rescue. This stretch of water, open to the wild Tasman Sea, can be extremely inhospitable in bad weather. Before returning to safety we noticed that the whales were milling about seemingly uncertain of which way to go. There was a lot of spyhopping, when whales pop their head out of the water and peer around. This behavior is thought to be used to search the horizon for navigation clues.

It was suggested that the large whale which had died may have been the leader of the pod, leaving the survivors to select a new leader. Obviously they wanted to head out to sea and avoid the dangers of the shoreline.

We were invited to join the wildlife biologist and veterinarian to examine the carcasses of the two whales that had died. My wife Penny, an operating room nurse, assisted at the autopsy.

One of the whales was a very old female and the other a middle-aged male. After a very lengthy and detailed examination, various whales experts surmised that the pod had probably followed a large school of squid and become disoriented in the confines of the bay.

Being a pelagic species, pilot whales are accustomed to navigating hundreds of miles offshore using a combination of echolocation and the Earth's electro-magnetic field. Their sonar can be confused by the type of geography present in Great Oyster Bay. The gently shallowing beach with rocky bluffs on each side is known as a classic whale trap. The whales traveled north in their traditional migratory pattern straight into the trap. They then took three days to figure out their escape route. Along the way they stranded twice. The two that died probably became exhausted from the struggle and stress of the strandings.

The way in which the rescued whales rushed to rejoin their pod clearly demonstrated that they were not committing suicide, once suggested as the reason for such strandings. pilot whales are a particularly social species; it is now thought that the distress cries of stranded whales cause others to attempt to come to their aid. This can result in waves of would-be rescuers getting into difficulty.

In some strandings, hundreds of pilot whales have died.

While we were working on the autopsy, an aircraft chartered by the Wildlife Branch of the Tasmanian state government flew overhead to look for the pod. A thorough search along the coast failed to find any trace of the whales and it was presumed that they had finally swum to freedom.

We were privileged to be in the right place at the right time to help these whales. Our time with them has led us along a fascinating path of research and discovery, including the making of a documentary video and the meeting of new friends.

Many of the people we have met, with whom we shared the story and videotape of our experience rescuing these pilot whales, have also had their lives positively changed forever by interactions with whales. ⊴

Whale Tales Glossary

Whale Words:

Baleen - comb-like plates in some whales' mouths which strain their food from a mouthful of water

Breach - when a cetacean jumps out of the water

Bioluminescence - plankton glowing at night when stimulated

Cetacean - dolphins, porpoises, and whales

Click-training - whale-produced underwater sounds which reflect off objects to inform cetaceans about what's around them (food, obstacles, relatives, and so on)

Dorsal fin - the fin in the center of a marine animal's back

Fluke - the tail fin of a cetacean

Pectoral fin - the side fin, like our arm, on a marine animal

Resident orca - fish-eating killer whales

Rorqual - those baleen whales with pleated, expandable throat pouches

Rostrum - the head, near the blowholes, of a whale

Saddle patch - greyish-white markings by the dorsal fin of an orca. They are unique, like a fingerprint

Sounding - when a cetacean dives deeply

Spout - the exhalation when a cetacean surfaces

Spyhopping -when a whale is vertical in the water, its head in the air, so it can look around

Super pod - several pods of orcas gathered, this is when they greet each other and mating occurs

Tail lobbing - slapping the water's surface with the tail

Transient orca - the marine mammal-eating killer whales

Whale Tales Glossary

Nautical words:

Dinghy - a small boat, often towed behind a larger boat

Ketch - a sailboat with two masts, where the shorter mast is behind and mounted ahead of the rudder post

Port side - the left hand side of the boat, when facing forward

Schooner - a sail boat with two masts, the shorter mast ahead

Sloop - a sailboat with one mast and two sails, a main and a jib

Starboard side - the right-hand side of the boat, when facing forward

Steerage way - when a boat is moving through the water and the rudder will direct the boat's course

Spinnaker - a large, often colorful sail, flown at the front of the boat for sailing off the wind

Acknowledgments

This book would not be here without the support, involvement, and power of many people. Virtually everyone I have spoken with about *Whale Tales* in the past year and a half has been a positive part of the process, from The Whale Museum to the woman at the insurance company; from dear old friends to strangers around the world; from the book distribution business to J-Pod itself (of the southern resident orca population).

I have needed and received a great deal of assistance. The staff at The Whale Museum has been there from start to finish. The idea for this book was hatched one evening after a slide show I presented at the Museum. Susan Key, Jon Luke, and I were talking and agreed that people who have had interactions with whales would probably be interested in sharing them, and other people might well be eager to read about those experiences. Thus, *Whale Tales* was born.

I was given use of the Museum's name and mailing list for the original publicity to let folks know that I wanted to hear from them. Beth Helstein reviewed the first transcription of the stories and the final manuscript of the book. Rich Osborne wrote some wonderful words for the Introduction. Polly Carr was excited to include *Whale Tales* in her National Endowment for the Arts and Humanities Story Telling series. Albert Shepard assisted me in developing an educational program to accompany *Whale Tales* readings. Everyone else at The Whale Museum has been interested in the book's progress as well.

The good people at the Center for Whale Research patiently answered my questions and encouraged me to follow through on completing the book.

Bruce Conway, book designer, introduced me to the wonder of working with digital photos and helped immensely.

Tillie, Thatch, Jon, Marshall, and the friends at Heartworks were always glad to see me when I came to use their telephone and copy machine.

Lee and Tal Sturdivant deserve more thanks than words on paper, providing continual coaching, and many meals, as this book grew from a pea-brained idea into real reality. I think Lee knew all along that self-publishing would be the way for *Whale Tales*.

People experienced in the worlds of whales and books offered advice and encouragement: Ken Balcomb, Terry Domico, Richard Ellis, Susan Eyerly, Howard Garrett, Jim Nollman and Jonathan White. Friends took the time to read and comment on the manuscript, including Sherri Byington, Judith Carter, Joann Weaver, as well as Beth, Jim, Lee, Marshall, and Susan.

As they have for years, my sailmakers, Susan and Peter Risser at San Juan Canvas, welcomed me into their oasis, where they shared their love of people as well as garden fresh vegetables and the wonderful humor of goofy jokes.

Ian Byington at By Design did a masterful job not only of editing, laying out, and designing *Whale Tales*, but also of making my project important in his life. Ian had the style, grace, and wit to keep me motivated to do my best.

Mary Wondra, Pat and Henry Meacham, and Darol Streib: with love, humor, and a belief in what I was doing, very generously loaned me the money to publish and promote *Whale Tales: Human Interactions With Whales, Volume One*.

Finally, this book would not exist without the contributions of those people who shared their stories. I am grateful for the time they took to tell me these tales, revise the transcribed story, and respond to several additional mailings. *Whale Tales* is their book.

Peter J. Fromm
San Juan Island, Washington
September, 1995

About the Author

Peter J. Fromm has been deeply involved with nature and the outdoors all his life: exploring caves, climbing mountains and rocks, running rivers, ski touring, bicycle touring and racing, backpacking, sea kayaking, and sailing.

While a student at Ohio University in Athens (BFA in Photography, 1971), Peter coordinated the activities for Earth Day, 1970. As a graduate student at the University of Oregon in Eugene (MS in Audio-Visual Communication combined with Outdoor Recreation/Education, 1974), Peter was active with the Outdoor Program's unique philosophy of recreation leadership, and the development of the multi-image (slide show) medium.

After graduating, Peter chose to learn to sail and moved to Bellingham, Washington. He has raced and cruised on more than one hundred and fifteen different boats in several parts of the world.

Since 1979, "Uwila," a custom, 1961, wooden, thirty-foot, double-ended yawl has been his full-time home. In the first nine months of 1995, "Uwila" was underway on 124 days. A licensed Master, he has worked for three years as captain and naturalist on whale watching boats.

Peter's primary profession, since 1970, has been photography, with a wide range of assignments and credits.

Peter J. Fromm's home base is in the San Juan Islands of Washington state.

Whale Tales is his first book.

About the Author

Peter J. Fromm has been deeply involved with nature and the outdoors all his life: exploring caves, climbing mountains and rocks, running rivers, ski touring, bicycle touring and racing, backpacking, sea kayaking, and sailing.

While a student at Ohio University in Athens (BFA in Photography, 1971), Peter coordinated the activities for Earth Day, 1970. As a graduate student at the University of Oregon in Eugene (MS in Audio-Visual Communication combined with Outdoor Recreation/Education, 1974), Peter was active with the Outdoor Program's unique philosophy of recreation leadership, and the development of the multi-image (slide show) medium.

After graduating, Peter chose to learn to sail and moved to Bellingham, Washington. He has raced and cruised on more than one hundred and fifteen different boats in several parts of the world.

Since 1979, "Uwila," a custom, 1961, wooden, thirty-foot, double-ended yawl has been his full-time home. In the first nine months of 1995, "Uwila" was underway on 124 days. A licensed Master, he has worked for three years as captain and naturalist on whale watching boats.

Peter's primary profession, since 1970, has been photography, with a wide range of assignments and credits.

Peter J. Fromm's home base is in the San Juan Islands of Washington state.

Whale Tales is his first book.

Index

Schedule Readings:

Peter J. Fromm is available for readings from *Whale Tales*. He has prepared an accompanying educational program about the changing relationship between whales and humans. When you wish to schedule an appearance for Peter, please contact him at the numbers below.

Call for Stories:

If you have the story of an interaction with a whale, dolphin or porpoise to contribute for a future volume of *Whale Tales*, please contact Peter at the numbers below, he will call you back to record your tale. If we use your story, you will receive a complimentary copy of the book. Photographs, videos, and illustrations are also welcomed for both *Whale Tales* books and the educational programs. Thanks!

Peter J. Fromm
Whale Tales Press
PO Box 865
Friday Harbor, WA 98250 USA

www.whaletales.com

360-378-8378

1-800-669-3950

The author uurges you to learn about and support
The Whale Museum's
Orca Adoption Program
Friday Harbor, Washington

Adopt an Orca and join The Whale Museum.
Get involved in protecting the orcas! Your symbolic adoption is a way to support ongoing education and field studies about the orcas.

Only 94 resident orcas ply the waters of Puget Sound and the southern British Columbia. These whales were once hunted and captured for display in marine parks. Between 1965 and 1976, sixty whales were removed or died in captures much like the one depicted in the movie, "Free Willy."

Orcas are unique beings.
Researchers at The Whale Museum and the Center for Whale Research, both in Friday Harbor, Washington, have been studying these wild animals in their natural habitat since 1974. Each orca can be identified by the shape and size of its dorsal fin and the black & white markings beneath and behind the fin, called the "saddle patch." Each animal has been given a pod identification number and a common name which reflects a bit of its heritage, personality, or circumstances of its discovery.

Orca adoptions make great gifts!
As an alternative to consumerism, an orca adoption is welcomed by all ages. Simple, thoughtful and fun, it's a great gift to receive. When you give an orca adoption, your contribution supports the non-profit work of The Whale Museum and the Center for Whale Research.

The whales of J-, K- and L-Pods could use your help to ensure their long-term well-being. Problems such as noise pollution from motor-powered vessels, habitat loss, and declining fish populations all need further study—and solutions.

To place an order, write or call:
The Whale Museum
P.O. Box 945
Friday Harbor, WA 98250 USA
1-800-946-7227

The Whale Museum is a center for environmental education and marine research.

It was created in 1979 through the efforts of more than four hundred volunteers. The Museum seeks, through education and research, to promote responsible stweardship of whales and the marine ecosystems upon which they, and we, depend.